PARABLE WISDOM

SPIRITUAL AWAKENING

IN THE TEACHINGS OF JESUS

By

Theodore J. Nottingham

Published by
Theosis Books
www.theosisbooks.com
© 2010 by Theodore J. Nottingham
All rights reserved.

ISBN 096649606X

Cover Art Bethanie at Sunrise

Printed in the United States of America.

PARABLE WISDOM

Table of Contents

Preface to the Second Edition

The Parable is a kind of language that seeks to bridge our ordinary way of thinking and understanding with spiritual wisdom. We do not have a language to speak of spiritual matters, so the parable and its imagery is a conduit for us to reveal sacred teaching so that we can be impacted by the power of the Divine in our lives. In Matthew 11, we are told: "The secrets of the Kingdom of Heaven have been given to you but not to them." Surely this is not a matter of favoritism. The Anointed One further explains that "whoever has will be given in abundance, but whoever does not have, even that will be taken away."

In that context, we are being told that whoever has opened themselves to the "secrets of the Kingdom" will receive more. But whoever does not have any interest in spiritual matters and rejects God's teachings, even that emptiness will be taken away from them. This calls us to seek to understand this critically important form of teaching which uses our ordinary everyday life and imagery to explain the deep things of Spirit. There is not question here about taking anything literally. The parables represent and point to something else.

Most of the time, we are left to our own prayerful openness to Spirit to understand what sacred scripture is telling us. But in some cases, the Christ gives us the codes and reveals to us what he is saying to us. The images are not about farmers or seeds, but about each of us.

Introduction

In the parables of Jesus, we find a timeless spiritual teaching that can make all things new in the heart, mind, and soul of each person. They can cause people to move from the darkness of self-absorption to the light of active unconditional love. This *metanoia*, this renewal and transformation is the hope for humanity.

The religion that grew out of the teachings of Jesus of Nazareth has had an often schizophrenic relationship to its origins. As a result, in this twenty-first century, many in our day have left the institutional Church and the dogmas of Christianity. They have also put aside the words of the Christ. Great numbers of these individuals have gone on to seek meaning, truth, spiritual awakening through other teachings. But in rejecting the teachings of Jesus along with the religion, it might be said that "the baby was thrown out with the bath water".

Many of these words have seeped into our culture over the centuries and become associated with ideas and ways of living that have nothing to do with their original meaning. These teachings of holy wisdom are associated with judgmentalism, rejection, intolerance, abuse, narrow-mindedness, even superstition. Yet, despite their misuse across these two millennia, individuals in every generation have encountered the divine light within these words and have been transformed psychologically and spiritually.

The reader will find in the presentation of these parables interpretive keys which transcend rigid theologies and assumed meanings that often bury their true content. The very nature of parabolic teaching is through the use of metaphor and therefore can never be boxed into a literalistic interpretation which has been the death-knell of so much biblical teaching. As the apostle said, *"The letter kills but the spirit gives life."* The teachings of Jesus have been hijacked far too long by those who do not live them out and do not follow their map to authentic enlightenment and awakening to the Presence of God. This book is offered to the reader in an effort to bring to light some of the transforming wisdom revealed to humanity so long ago and so desperately needed again today. May you, the reader, find for yourself that which will fill your life with new understanding and lift you into a higher place within, guiding you into becoming the person you were always called to be.

THE PATH OF RETURN
THE PARABLE OF THE PRODIGAL SON
Luke 15: 11-24

Then Jesus said, 'There was a man who had two sons. The younger of them said to his father, "Father, give me the share of the property that will belong to me." So he divided his property between them. A few days later the younger son gathered all he had and travelled to a distant country, and there he squandered his property in dissolute living. When he had spent everything, a severe famine took place throughout that country, and he began to be in need. So he went and hired himself out to one of the citizens of that country, who sent him to his fields to feed the pigs. He would gladly have filled himself with the pods that the pigs were eating; and no one gave him anything. But when he came to himself he said, "How many of my father's hired hands have bread enough and to spare, but here I am dying of hunger! I will get up and go to my father, and I will say to him, 'Father, I have sinned against heaven and before you; I am no longer worthy to be called your son; treat me like one of your hired hands.' " So he set off and went to his father. But while he was still far off, his father saw him and was filled with compassion; he ran and put his arms around him and kissed him. Then the son said to him, "Father, I have sinned against heaven and before you; I am no longer worthy to be called your son." But the father said to his slaves, "Quickly, bring out a robe—the best one—and put it on him; put a ring on his finger and sandals on his feet. And get the fatted calf and kill it, and let us eat and celebrate; for this son of mine was dead and is alive again; he was lost and is found!" And they began to celebrate.

In this parable, we have the great privilege of witnessing what may be the mightiest teaching of Jesus, the culmination of why he came and what he is trying to communicate to us. This is the parable of parables, the gospel within the gospel. It is also an opportunity to see how glorious these teachings are, how rich and full, and inexhaustible, even in a lifetime of study. They are so much more than what appears on the surface as simple storytelling. To experience the treasures of wisdom in this teaching, we need to plunge deep.

First and foremost, we must understand that this parable is not about someone else. This is not about a "prodigal" (wasteful) son. The word *prodigal* is not even mentioned in the Bible. Yet for centuries, we have called this parable "the story of the prodigal son". The fact is that this is your story, my story. This is the map showing us how to reconnect with spirit, with our deeper selves in spite of our past mistakes.

The parable begins with, **"Then Jesus said,"** so we need to put it in context. Jesus has been with what the Bible calls sinners, with people who know little of God. Sin means in Greek *missing the mark*, missing your purpose in life. This is why so many people die in despair and the gospels are called "good news" because they reveal a way out of such despair.

So Jesus tells the parable to the Pharisees, the religious people who frown upon his companionship with humanity. He then tells them the story of the lost sheep and the "rejoicing in heaven" for that one lost sheep, more than for the ninety-nine who have no need of repentance. Here we find a clue to the profundity of this mighty teaching. The Greek does not state that the ninety-nine have no need of repentance. It states that the ninety-nine believe *they have no need for repentance.* It is not a case of re-ligious people who are so good that they have nothing in their behavior for which to repent. The issue is that they do not feel any need to repent, to change their ways, to turn around and live in another manner. They are the self-righteous. They are the self-satisfied. In other words, they represent the human condition so filled with pride, ignorance, and forgetfulness. This is the backdrop for the parable of the prodigal son.

In order to break out of that state of blindness, which misses the whole point of what we are called to do in or-der to connect with our deeper spirit and with God, it is necessary to begin by not being one of those ninety-nine who believe they are just fine and do not think they need to change in any way.

The parable opens with the son -- you and me -- saying to God, **"Give me my share of the estate."** This statement can be translated as" "Thank you very much, God, for my life, for my talents, for my energy, and goodbye." Does that not reveal how we take for granted all the wonder of life and just use it for ourselves? We generally believe that we are here merely to take care of ourselves, forgetting the big picture, forgetting our origins, forgetting that there is something else to be done here besides just satisfying ourselves. We have forgotten that we have been given life for a purpose, for God's purpose.

Just like that son, each of us takes our life as our own to do with as we wish and go off to seek self-satisfaction. The teaching tells us that he sets out for, in the modern version, a *distant country* unlike the old translation, a *far country*, one in which we do not belong. That far country is not a long distance away. It is all around us. It is the country, the culture, the world as we know it, one in which there is no God, nothing is sacred, everyone is out for themselves -- the world of greed that has done so much damage to humanity.

We are told that he squandered his wealth. This is not about fiscal responsibility. "Squandering wealth" means wasting that which God has given us. Every day that we live in anxiety, anger, and impatience is squandered when it is lived that way. That is at the heart of the teachings of Jesus: the call to awaken.

This day is the day that we do not want to squander because it will not come back to us. We have to be present now to our existence before it is over.

"And after he had spent everything," or in other words, after we have used up all our energy, **"there was a severe famine"**. This was not a potato famine, nor any kind of food famine. This was a *spiritual famine* in the far country. We are living in a spiritual famine now in this world.

Each of us is in a spiritual famine if we are not tuning back to Spirit, to God, to goodness and light. If we let ourselves go adrift in the far country of a secular world where there is no God.

"And so he was in need." Surely all of us have been in need at some point -- in need of God's presence, of meaning, fulfillment and peace. All of us need to be brought back to that center in ourselves where there is peace and joy regardless of circumstances. The prodigal son was in such a need that he **"hired himself out"**.

Here we have a wonderful example of how Jesus teaches. We read that **"he hired himself out and he was sent to the fields to feed pigs."** Pigs were used in ancient times as food for idols so they were considered especially unclean.

The son (or child of God who has wandered so far from the source) finds himself necessarily engaged in dealing with the lowest and most impure of activities. We are told that he would have been happy to eat the husks left over from the unclean animals. That is how far he fell from his birthright. This image represents the misery, confusion, pain, hopelessness and meaninglessness of an existence disconnected from the spiritual dimension.

We have all tasted such a life at some point, whether occasioned by circumstances or by our own mistakes, or perhaps as a result of drifting along without paying attention. So Jesus takes his teaching into our deepest places where we most need God. We are told, **"But no one gave him anything."** We are not going to find what we need spiritually except through the process contained in this parable. We can find a few clues from a guru or some half-truths in the self-improvement movement. But if we really want the knowledge that is going to change our lives, it is to be found here.

We are told that *he came to his senses* or *when he came to his senses* in most translations. But the original Greek states **"when he came into himself,"** when he *remembered who he was* while digging in that mud with the pigs. In other words, when we finally become conscious of our deepest self and how far we have traveled from it and how much we have sold out, to what extent we are no longer the person we truly are, then we know how far we have betrayed our authentic identity.

He remembered who he was. He said to himself, **"How many of my father's hired hands have food to spare?"** Consider how this metaphor speaks to us. Here we are children of God in this universe and those who are not even members of the family, the servants and the hired help, are doing well while we are groveling in the mud of wrong living. And so he says, "**I will set out and go back to my father. I will set out and go back to my father.**" This is the axis on which everything changes. We are not Christians because we come to church. We are not Christians because we were born into the religion. We are Christians because we are conscious of the reality of God and want to reestablish that relationship. We make a decision which unifies us around that purpose to reclaim our deeper identity, our spiritual self.

"**And I will say to him, I have sinned against heaven and against you. I'm no longer worthy to be called your child.**" This is the manifestation of the cornerstone for any authentic spiritual awakening: *humility*. We recognize our failings, our weaknesses, our mistakes, those times when we did not behave appropriately. Such humbling self-awareness is the first step on to the journey back to God. If we are self-satisfied, we cannot get on that path of return to God. Only through honest self-awareness can we begin again.

Verse 20 tells us that "**he got up and went to his father.**" Each of us has to get up and head back to God, has to rise up out of the dust of our mistakes and "return to God." This is obviously not a physical journey. It is spiritual and psychological. The "return" is experienced in commitments such as: "I will not behave this way anymore," "I will struggle against these habits, these imitations, these wounds that have created the false self and taken me away from God."

Now we come upon the ultimate revelation. There are many great teachings across the centuries given to humanity, but no one ever taught this: "**While he was still a long way off,**" while you and I are still in our sad state of affairs and are barely managing to turn to God, while we are just beginning to make a step on that journey, something extraordinary happens. "**His father saw him.**" God responds to our desire to return to God!

Here Jesus reveals the character of the Divine. *God runs to us.* God doesn't just see us. God runs toward us. As the saying goes: Take one step towards God, God will take ten steps towards you. Jesus is telling us that just our desire to find God will cause God run to us and embrace us. This is why we have joy as Christians because that is the God revealed to us by Jesus.

Then come the metaphors -- put *on the best robe, sandals for his feet* -- all these ancient images that are the celebration of spirit when we become aware of our need for God, when we remember that we are spirit incarnated in matter, when our identity is no longer what the far country tells us it is, and when we realize that we are a child of the Almighty, loved beyond all understanding by the One who is unconditional love.

Then we read these mighty words, "**For this son of mine was dead and is alive again**" -- meaning dead in spirit, as we surely are in that far country where nothing is sacred, where there is no mystery, and certainly no humility. This parable invites us to take the path homeward, to come alive again in spirit. It teaches us that we will be found when we know that we are lost. This is the heart of the gospel, which calls each of us to that life-giving Truth.

2

GOOD SOIL
THE PARABLE OF THE SOWER
Matthew 13: 1-9

That same day Jesus went out of the house and sat beside the lake. Such great crowds gathered around him that he got into a boat and sat there, while the whole crowd stood on the beach. And he told them many things in parables, saying: 'Listen! A sower went out to sow. And as he sowed, some seeds fell on the path, and the birds came and ate them up. Other seeds fell on rocky ground, where they did not have much soil, and they sprang up quickly, since they had no depth of soil. But when the sun rose, they were scorched; and since they had no root, they withered away. Other seeds fell among thorns, and the thorns grew up and choked them. Other seeds fell on good soil and brought forth grain, some a hundredfold, some sixty, some thirty. Let anyone with ears listen!'

In many parables we are left to figuring them out on our own, which is why teachers down through the ages have said that this effort requires careful preparation. Here we have one of the few parables for which Jesus provides an actual explanation. In doing so, he offers us a key to deciphering the teaching.

We have been given the tools to understand what has been encapsulated in these simple images and sent down through time so that all people in all cultures can grasp the revelation of this divine wisdom and apply it to their lives. A parable is nothing less than a conduit of meaning, a way to enable our materialistic minds to grasp spiritual truth. A parable is a bridge between different kinds of thinking and different modes of understanding.

"A farmer went out to sow." Every culture can understand that statement. We need to understand it spiritually. In that light, those words translate to: *Christ came from God with a teaching.* The seed is the Word -- the teaching, spiritual understanding. This teaching from the Anointed One lands on different kinds of soils. Most of us can understand that if a seed falls on hard earth, on a path going through the woods or in a field, it cannot break through and begin to grow. The Gospel of Luke tells us that, on this path, the seed is *trampled on.* These are symbolic images of one way that the teachings of Christ are received.

How many people are there who are not in the least bit interested in spiritual things? When Jesus explains this form of receptivity which he names "hard path," he says: **"Birds of the air came and picked them up."** In another gospel, he says, **"The evil one removed it."** In the language of parables, birds are often human thoughts, our own thoughts. If we are full of all kinds of thoughts and cannot discern good from evil, then the seed just vanishes in the chaos of our minds. This is one kind of receiving.

Another kind of receiving is expressed as on *rocky ground where there is some soil.* Unlike the hard path, the seed can get through the soil. But there is no depth. As Jesus says, when such persons first hear spiritual ideas, they rejoice, but the first time they must apply them in real circumstances, they walk away. In the Greek we are told that such a person is *offended when persecutions occur on account of the Word.*

There are people who love to gather knowledge and information but then never apply any of it to their lives. A difference exists between their knowledge and their character. Peter was like that. Despite those years with Jesus at his side, when the test came he could not rise to the occasion and *be* what he had learned. That is the great struggle for all of us: To take that knowledge and apply it to our lives in transformative ways. If someone states that they have been to church for many years, but they cannot tolerate "that guy over there," they are failing to apply the teachings. That is rocky ground and the teaching is lost to us.

God is present to us, but we do not want to make the necessary efforts. We cannot face ourselves. It is rocky ground because the teachings can only come alive when we actually apply them to our personal issues. We are dealing here with living truth, living wisdom and to walk away from it is to be among the "dead who are burying the dead."

Another way that we receive spiritual teaching is described as *thorny ground.* We value the teaching. It impacts our lives. We cherish it. We try to live it out *but there are other things in our soil,* other interests that compete with the seed, drawing energy and nutrition away from spiritual teaching as the center of our lives.

Jesus is describing three ways of receiving transforming teaching:
1. The hard path where nothing even gets in -- this is much of the human condition.
2. The rocky ground where the teaching cannot take root because it is not being lived out in daily life.
3. The thorny ground where the teaching competes with other things in our lives and does not have the priority that will give it power.

The teaching does not end there for it is not about three different kinds of people. This parable is about different places *within us.* Each of us has that hard path that is too prideful or arrogant to receive spiritual wisdom. Each of us has other interests that drag us away from enlightenment and new life. Each of us must ask the question: How am I receiving this wisdom in my life?

Finally, Jesus speaks to us of the *good soil,* which is also in each of us. That good soil is deep, soft, receptive, accepting and it is purified or purged. There are no weeds in it. There are no competing distractions that will divert the nutrition. It is all focused on the divine seed. The word for "good earth" in Latin is *humus*. *Humus* means humility, and such is the good earth where the teaching can grow, blossom, transform us, and produce a miracle yield. In a person with true humility, there is nothing hard that rejects the Word because we no longer come first. Openness, simplicity, quietness, receptivity – this is the good soil. All of us are capable of that kind of receptivity. This is why humility is the cornerstone of Christian spirituality. We cannot progress without it.

If our life is miserable, if our relationships are falling apart, let us look at what kind of "ground" we are providing for these teachings to work in us, for the rooting of these teachings, for their valuation and application. We are assured that, if we become good soil, then the crop will yield a hundred fold, meaning that unimaginable blessings will flow into our lives. And what is that crop? It is who we become as we live in this consciousness of God, in this application of the wisdom of God.

Jesus says, "**Blessed are your eyes and ears who understand this,**" because many prophets came before, many bright people, many spiritual seekers down through time who did not understand this teaching. Blessed are we when we understand these things. This is heart of Gospel.

Jesus reveals humanity to itself and how we can change, how we can find the deeper, better part of ourselves that can make all the difference. So this parable, like all the others, is a map, an instruction booklet, a code for us to figure out and apply. Those who have ears, let them hear.

3

THE ELEVENTH HOUR
THE PARABLE OF THE LABORERS
Matthew 20: 1-16

'For the kingdom of heaven is like a landowner who went out early in the morning to hire laborers for his vineyard. After agreeing with the laborers for the usual daily wage, he sent them into his vineyard. When he went out about nine o'clock, he saw others standing idle in the market-place; and he said to them, "You also go into the vineyard, and I will pay you whatever is right." So they went. When he went out again about noon and about three o'clock, he did the same. And about five o'clock he went out and found others standing around; and he said to them, "Why are you standing here idle all day?" They said to him, "Because no one has hired us." He said to them, "You also go into the vineyard." When evening came, the owner of the vineyard said to his manager, "Call the laborers and give them their pay, beginning with the last and then going to the first." When those hired about five o'clock came, each of them received the usual daily wage. Now when the first came, they thought they would receive more;

but each of them also received the usual daily wage. And when they received it, they grumbled against the landowner, saying, "These last worked only one hour, and you have made them equal to us who have borne the burden of the day and the scorching heat." But he replied to one of them, "Friend, I am doing you no wrong; did you not agree with me for the usual daily wage? Take what belongs to you and go; I choose to give to this last the same as I give to you. Am I not allowed to do what I choose with what belongs to me? Or are you envious because I am generous?" So the last will be first, and the first will be last.'

The chapter opens with the words *"the kingdom of heaven is like"* which means that this teaching is a response to something that has happened before. If we look at chapter 19, it is clear that a great deal has gone before, namely the parable of the rich young man who comes up to Jesus and says, *"Master, how do I inherit eternal life?"*

In order to understand the parable, we must understand the context: the story of the rich young man who asks this great question. What is he asking? He is asking what everyone in their heart of hearts is asking: How do I find God? How do I relate to God? How do I develop relationship? How do I get help from a higher power? There are answers to these questions and they are not merely answers. They are an entry into personal experience of the reality of the living Spirit.

We are all the rich young man. He is not rich with cash, but with self-sufficiency. He tells Jesus, "I follow all the rules. I'm a religious person," and yet that is not enough. Jesus responds with the words, **"Sell all you have."** This is not about the furniture. He is not telling this person that the way to relate to God is to become a vagrant. If we become homeless, how are we going to help the homeless? This is the absurdity of literal interpretation. The reason that the teaching is encoded in parables is for us to think from a deeper place, a place we do not visit very often.

When the disciples hear that even this person who has been so religious and followed all the rules is given such a demanding teaching to leave everything he knows in order to discover something new, they exclaim in terror, **"Who then can be saved?"** It is in response to this question that Jesus shares his teaching. The parable is a response to the question, "How do I find God?"

A landowner wants to hire people to work in his vineyard. That landowner is God. Working in the vineyard is doing God's work, or more specifically, living the life that God wants us to live. This work is about being the kind of person that God wants us to be. Not all of us can "do" things. Some of us are wheelchair-bound so there are other ways to serve God in God's vineyard.

The story tells us that the landowner hires people at different times of the day. We find that, at the end of the day, the eleventh hour -- meaning five o'clock, one hour before quitting time -- he hires some more. He says to them, "**Why are you just standing there?**" The people who have been waiting all day long in the heat of the sun, who may not have had a meal on this day respond, "**No one will hire us.**" We need to understand this statement spiritually. These are people who want to do God's work, who want to know God, who want to live the spiritual life, who want to understand these teachings. They cannot find what they are looking for. How many of us are there in that position? There are many people who have gone to church for a lifetime and cannot find what they are looking for. Our world is full of lost people that no one will hire, no one will bring into the vineyard to rejoice at doing God's work.

True fulfillment is to find that invitation from God saying: *I need you to be part of my mission, whoever you are.* These are not simply people who are just hanging around not doing anything and, out of the blue, God calls them. They are looking for something even if it is late in the journey of life. When it comes time to pay everyone, the landowner does not first pay those who have been working all day. He specifically pays the last ones first. Why? So that the first ones can see what he is doing and when they see it, they become outraged just as each of us might be expected to feel. *"Wait a minute, I've been working all day long and you're going to pay them the same you're paying me?"* They, and we, expect more.

The point of this parable is that God blesses and graces all of us no matter how long we have worked. There are those who have worked all day long, those who have been in church for thirty years, perhaps have a certain sense of ownership, a certain pride that they should be in charge. They tell themselves: "We've done all the work. We've paid for all of this." This teaching from the savior states that it does not work that way in God's sight and that is offensive. Verse 15, in the average English translation, contains a watered down translation of the landowner's response: **"Don't I have the right to do what I want with my own money?"** The actual translation is: **"Why is your eye evil when I am good?"**

This statement of Jesus might be compared with another one from Matthew 6:22, **"The eye is the lamp of the body so if your eye is healthy, your whole body will be full of light but if your eye is unhealthy, your whole body will be full of darkness. If then the light in you is darkness, how great is that darkness if your spirit is darkened?"** *If your eye, your way of seeing is so unhealthy that when you see something good, you call it evil? How great is that darkness?*

In Mark chapter three, there is a reference to the "one sin that cannot be forgiven." Jesus says that this is the sin against the Holy Spirit. The Pharisees had accused him of being able to heal because he had a demon in him. In other words, the savior is doing something good, is giving God's love to someone in need, and the religious folks call it an evil act.

When we see good as evil, we can no longer recognize good and all is lost. Jesus says to these people who feel they deserve more than others because they have worked harder: *How can you question the generosity of God?* A God who will give the same love and blessing to you who have just begun your spiritual journey, a God who will give you as much grace and blessing as to the person who has been faithful for fifty years.

The people who have been waiting to be hired until the last minute are those who deal with a great deal of misery in their lives. Much of it may be self-produced through broken relationships, unemployment, and the inability to discover the right path in life for themselves. Yet despite all the mistakes and foolishness, God says to us: *As long as you want to accept my invitation and come into my vineyard, you receive as much as the greatest saint.* This is the kind of God Jesus reveals.

The disciples hear this and say, **"Who then can be saved?"** Their thinking is: we do all the right things and we are still not at the top of the list. Jesus responds by saying that **"for mortals it is impossible but for God, all things are possible."** This is an opportunity for every person to say "yes" to the invitation of God, to work together side by side with others to the glory of God.

"The first shall be last, the last shall be first." Why? Because if we expect and think we deserve to be first, we will find ourselves at the back of the line. But if we know ourselves and know what we need and how badly we need it, God places us at the head of the line for the receipt of divine blessing.

The Parable of the Laborers

4

LIGHT WITHIN
THE PARABLE OF THE TEN VIRGINS
Matthew 25: 1-13

'Then the kingdom of heaven will be like this. Ten bridesmaids took their lamps and went to meet the bridegroom. Five of them were foolish, and five were wise. When the foolish took their lamps, they took no oil with them; but the wise took flasks of oil with their lamps. As the bridegroom was delayed, all of them became drowsy and slept. But at midnight there was a shout, "Look! Here is the bridegroom! Come out to meet him." Then all those bridesmaids got up and trimmed their lamps. The foolish said to the wise, "Give us some of your oil, for our lamps are going out." But the wise replied, "No! there will not be enough for you and for us; you had better go to the dealers and buy some for yourselves." And while they went to buy it, the bridegroom came, and those who were ready went with him into the wedding banquet; and the door was shut. Later the other bridesmaids came also, saying, "Lord, lord, open to us." But he replied, "Truly I tell you, I do not know you." Keep awake therefore, for you know neither the day nor the hour.

We have before us what might be called a message in a bottle. Here are teachings from the Holy One dealing directly with matters of your life, hidden within the language of parable, the language of spiritual metaphor. So our job is to get to the core of what is being said.

We are told that ten bridesmaids took their lamps and went to meet the bridegroom. This is in the context of ancient eastern weddings which happened at night. The bridegroom would go through the town on his way to the bride, accompanied by people carrying torches. It was a great festivity and the banquet lasted for seven days. Here ends the connection with first century everyday life and this parable. Beneath it lies a mighty teaching.

The first clue to understanding the parable is to know that *we* are the bridesmaids. We are carrying lamps. What are these lamps? Looking through the Old Testament, we hear the Psalms saying: **"Lord, you are lamp unto my feet."** It is obviously a metaphor which refers to the fact that we carry the teaching which Jesus has brought to us. We believe in it in some way or other and we are on our way to meet the bridegroom who is Jesus himself.

The parable tells us that five bridesmaids were foolish and five were wise. The English word "wise" fails to translate what is being said. In the original Greek language, we have the word *phronimos* which has a different connotation. When Jesus says, **"I thank you father that you did not reveal these things to the wise but to children,"** he is using a different word, *sophos,* in a negative sense for those who are *wise in this world*. He uses this

26

other word, *phronimos*, when he talks about the builders who build on rock. They are wise and he defines what that means: **"Those who hear my teaching and act on it."**

So this expression translated as "wise" means something very specific and special. It means the quality required to be a follower of Jesus, the presence of mind, the ability to be conscious enough of what the right action is in the moment. This idea is contrasted with the word *foolish*. The Greek is *mori* from which we get the word moron. The foolish bridesmaids, who carry the teachings of Jesus, have no oil. They brought no oil with their lamp. They carry a teaching that does not penetrate into their lives and gives them light. Lamps are meant to give us light but they cannot do so by themselves.

We then find ourselves confronted with another metaphor: Oil. Oil in the Old Testament is found many times and is used for anointing priests and kings. The great vision of the prophet Zechariah pictures a lamp stand with two olive trees from which oil drips into the lamp stand and he hears the Word of the Lord saying, **"Not by power, not by might but by my spirit, says the Lord."** The word in Hebrew, *Maschiach*, which in Greek is *Christos*, means *the anointed one*, anointed with the spirit of God. So this little word "oil" is not about a flame in an old Aladdin's lamp. It deals with the issue of how, through our willpower, we apply the teachings of Jesus in our lives.

When there is no oil, the flame goes out. We can spend a lifetime in church, believe all these teachings, faithfully show up every Sunday and never apply them to our daily life. If we are angry and have heard the words of Jesus on that matter, yet choose to remain angry anyway, we have no oil for our lamps. We have no inner light. The prologue of the Gospel of John tells us: **"In him was life and he was the light of all people and the light shined in the darkness and the darkness did not understand**." Our life is lived in this darkness until we become illumined in our understanding by the application of these spiritual teachings.

If we live only by the senses and there is no God in our reality, we live in darkness. If we call ourselves Christians and believe all these wonderful ideas but never care to apply them to our personal issues, we are "foolish bridesmaids" whose lamps are going to go out at the wrong time. We are told not to judge, yet how many of us can stand up and say, "*I am free of criticizing others*"? Not one of us. This statement is not to make us feel guilty, but rather to make the point that the whole purpose of studying the teachings of Jesus is to make changes in our lives. We cannot remain the same and be a Christian.

We do not come into this world ready to be followers of Jesus. We have to make specific psychological efforts in our moment to moment choices. We are expected to make oil for ourselves, to go against the current of how we would naturally behave. So all of us know in our own particular ways, where it is that we need to be "making oil," where we need to be applying those things we say we believe in so that they might generate an organic transformation of who we are. An impatient person can become a patient human being. This is making oil for ourselves.

We are told that **"the bridegroom is delayed."** Think about that. Where is Jesus? We live our everyday ordinary life with all its ups and downs and God seems absent to your awareness. This is not because there is no God, but is due to the fact that we are not *present* to God. So the bridegroom is delayed. What happens as a result? The wise and the foolish get drowsy and fall asleep. "Sleep" in spiritual writings is a metaphor for our state of consciousness. In other words, sleep is a condition of our awareness in which God is not present. This is darkness. The world lives there and that is why the world is the way it is. That is why your life is the way it is.

We live in a state of sleep, unaware of the light of understanding that makes us new people, able to live in the will of God. If we "wake up" everything changes. We cannot change our outer circumstances but we can change ourselves. If we change ourselves, our outer circumstances begin to change as well. If we are cold and unpleasant to people, we do not have many friends. If we are good and kind, people will want to be around us.

Then we are told that something happens **"at the midnight hour."** At the darkest hour, at the time of crisis in our life, when we are in the hospital all alone and need to find that faith to get us through — that is our midnight hour. At the midnight hour, there was a shout, "*Look, here* *comes the bridegroom. Let's come and meet him."* So the brides-maids get up and the foolish ones find that their lamps have going out.

How do we make it through those hard times, those dark times? How do we make it through any part of our life and keep that lamp burning? Faith is not a static thing. We do not merely get it and keep it in our back pocket. Like oil, it is consumed. It has to be replenished. Each day there is something new because our God is a living God and these ancient teachings are forever new. They are life itself.

The wise bridesmaids say: *"No, we can't give you any of our oil. You have to go and buy some for your self."* This is not be-cause the bridesmaids are selfish. It is because we cannot give to someone else a relationship with Spirit. We can-not awaken someone else to the knowledge of God, to the power of their own inner potential. We each have to find that for ourselves. We have to have our own inner understanding, our light within. We cannot take it from somebody else.

The prophet Jeremiah said: *"Inspired by the spirit of God, one day, you shall all know me."* Ideally, people join together in community on Sundays so that each one can find their way to encounter with God, can create light within, be-cause these teachings awaken us spiritually. They free us from the way of life we have lived thoughtlessly outside of the Presence of God.

The bridesmaids who have no oil must go out and buy some. The parable tells us that while they were out, the bridegroom came. **"And those who were ready, went with him into the wedding banquet."** What does the "wedding banquet" represent? Union with God.

This saying is not about the afterlife. This teaching is for right now, today. Jesus came that we might have life abundantly, that we might live that banquet now, but we remain outside of that potential reality. The rest of that verse reads: **"and the door was shut."**

God does not shut the door on us. We shut the door on ourselves. We shut ourselves out of the kingdom of God, out of relationship with God by choosing to not live the teachings, by taking the easy way, by behaving any old way, by staying the same, by not creating light within through applying these teachings to our daily life.

The bridesmaids come back, they say, **"Lord, Lord, let us in. Open to us."** Truth Incarnate says to them, **"Truly, I tell you, I do not know you."** Again, it is not that God does not know us. It is that we do not know God. So Jesus tells us: **"Keep awake."** The purpose of the gospel is for each of us to know God, to have new understanding, to get into the wedding banquet, to live a life that has meaning and joy and purpose.

This is why the apostle Paul says: **"Forgetting what lies behind, I strain towards what lies ahead, seeking the prize that God has for me,"** that God has for each of us. If we want to be Christians, if we want to stay on this path, we must keep moving forward, renewing our efforts to be the people God wants us to be. Then we find that the door is wide open!

5

FORGIVENESS
THE PARABLE OF THE UNMERCIFUL SERVANT
Matthew 18: 21-35

'For this reason the kingdom of heaven may be compared to a king who wished to settle accounts with his slaves. When he began the reckoning, one who owed him ten thousand talents was brought to him; and, as he could not pay, his lord ordered him to be sold, together with his wife and children and all his possessions, and payment to be made. So the slave fell on his knees before him, saying, "Have patience with me, and I will pay you everything." And out of pity for him, the lord of that slave released him and forgave him the debt. But that same slave, as he went out, came upon one of his fellow-slaves who owed him a hundred denarii; and seizing him by the throat, he said, "Pay what you owe." Then his fellow-slave fell down and pleaded with him, "Have patience with me, and I will pay you." But he refused; then he went and threw him into prison until he should pay the debt. When his fellow-slaves saw what had happened, they were greatly distressed, and they went and reported to their lord all that had taken place. Then his lord summoned him and said

to him, "You wicked slave! I forgave you all that debt because you pleaded with me. Should you not have had mercy on your fellow-slave, as I had mercy on you?" And in anger his lord handed him over to be tortured until he should pay his entire debt. So my heavenly Father will also do to every one of you, if you do not forgive your brother or sister from your heart.'

Chapter 18 of Matthew begins with the famous statement of Jesus saying, *"Bring the little ones unto me and unless you are like one of these, you cannot enter the kingdom."* But then he goes on to say that the term "these little one" does not refer to children, but rather to disciples. It refers to those who are seeking God. Why are they called little ones?

Clearly, anyone who wants be a Christian must travel the road of humility. In a world full of arrogance and pride and search for power, those who claim to be Christian must be like the little ones. Peter asks him, "How many times should I forgive?" In the ancient Jewish teachings, the rabbis actually had a number -- three times. That was the rule. You forgive somebody three times. The fourth time, forgiveness is no longer necessary. In the rest of the world, there was no talk of forgiving. Not once.

So Peter says, *"How many times? Seven times?"* He did not merely pick a number out of the air. Seven is a special number, a profoundly symbolic number. In the teachings of ancient Israel, it means *wholeness, completion, fullness.* In other words, one is to forgive always. But the Master goes further. One translation reads "seventy-seven." Another translation reads "seventy times seven." It is a confusing Greek word. Does that mean 490 times? On the 491st time, it is okay to hate, to get revenge? Of course not. Here is what Jesus is saying: Infinity squared, that is how much we forgive.

This teaching takes place in the context of a chapter where Jesus is giving us instructions on dealing with people who have offended another person in a spiritual community. Jesus is not saying, "Don't worry about it. Just forgive him." This is not what the parable is about. In fact, right before the parable, he gives us specific instructions. If someone has offended you in the spiritual community, go to them, try to talk to them, bring them back into some degree of spiritual understanding. If that does not work, take two witnesses with you as in the days of Moses and try again. If that does not work, take the issue to the whole community and if the person refuses to enter into the ways of God again, let them become **"like a Gentile and a tax collector."** What does that translate into? Let them be like someone who has no interest in God and the ways of God. The Master is saying, in other words -- Let them go live in outer darkness.

In the parable of the unmerciful servant, Jesus tells us that there was a king who wanted to settle his accounts. This image ought to get our attention. Someday, our Creator is going to want to settle accounts and everyone who has a conscience knows that they have got a little something that is not right in the sight of the Holy One. In the parable, we find a person just like us, a servant of the Master who owes him 10,000 talents. Scholars tell us that one talent was equal to 6000 drachmas, which was equal to 15 years wages for a laborer at the time. It only took 900 talents to get the annual tax income of Herod the Great's lands. What is Jesus saying? The current fiscal translation is $16 million. In other words, we are dealing with a debt that cannot possibly be paid. In other words, this is a picture of each of us in front of God with a debt we cannot pay. In each one of our lives, we have failed the Holy One.

The whole point of becoming like Christ is to purify the heart, and how we have failed on the way. We cannot possibly pay back what we owe to Ultimate Goodness. Each one has failed. Our humanity is expressed in that servant who falls to his knees and says, *"Please give me time. Be patient with me. I'll pay it back."* The parable tells us that the king took pity on him. The more literal translation is: *"He had a gut level feeling of compassion for him, for you and for me."* He not only gave him time, he cancelled the debt. God cancels the debt we cannot pay. This is the revelation of Jesus. This is the good news. God takes pity on us, no matter who we are, no matter what we have done and cancels it.

Now the king was going to sell him into slavery, him and his family and everything he owned in order to pay off the impossible debt. This also has a symbolic meaning. "Selling into slavery" means that our failures, our weaknesses, our sins, our mistakes, our ungodly ways *enslave* us. As long as we are caught in that debt of not living as Christ has shown us, we are slaves and that cancellation frees us to live a new life.

So this man with his canceled debt **"went off."** We have here a seemingly a simple line, but when we are reading sacred scripture, we must take our time because those three words, "he went off" actually means *he left the presence of God.* Even after this incredible, miraculous cancellation of all debt, he leaves the Holy presence. He goes away from God. And what does he do? He runs into another servant who says, **"Please be patient. Give me time to pay you back what I owe to you."** Now this individual owes him a few denarius which come to approximately fourteen dollars. The man was just forgiven a sixteen million dollar debt. But having left the presence of the Holy One (in other words, having forgotten God), this man grabs him by the throat and says, "Pay me back." And that servant begging for mercy speaks exactly the same words that he spoke to the king. This is a clue to the teaching. How often do we judge other people for the very things that we have done? How shameful. How wrong in the eyes of God.

There is one thing in particular that Jesus could not stand. He was tolerant of everyone. He broke all the rules. He forgave the prostitute. He cared for the lepers that nobody would go near. But he could not tolerate the hypocrites. Again and again, he cries out: **"You hypocrites!"** and he says that in a particular way in Luke: **"How can you judge the dust in your neighbor's eye when there is a plank in your own?"** This is the perennial wisdom "Know thyself." In learning to know ourselves, we discover the position we are in before God. And when we know that, what happens? We become "like a little one." We become humble. We no longer dare to judge others because we know our position before God. That is the process of becoming a disciple of Jesus.

The wicked servant who failed to show mercy to another person who owed even less than he did is brought back before the king. The parable tells us that the other servants were outraged. The ancient fathers interpreted this verse in this manner: *"These are angels, you see, who let God know what has happened."* Nothing passes unseen before the eyes of God, not anything done on the national scene nor in the privacy of our secret world. So this servant is brought back before the king and the king says, **"You wicked servant. Shouldn't you have had mercy on this fellow servant as I had on you?"**

Should we not have had mercy on our fellow human beings just as God had on us? Next time we judge, next time we refuse to forgive, may that sentence of Jesus haunt us: **"Shouldn't you have had mercy as I had on you?"** God has mercy on us whether we know it or not and surely we know there has been mercy in our lives, and therefore we are called to forgive as well.

The king sends the wicked servant to the jailers and the torturers to make him pay the whole debt back, which of course is never going to happen. So the ancient fathers considered this an image of eternal damnation. Yet, the statement is not as intense as what follows. The last words in this parable given by Jesus are: **"This is how**

my heavenly father will treat each of you if you do not forgive your brother or sister from your heart."

We like to think of Jesus as a wonderful, sweet guy. This is an inaccurate picture. He was a man of fire, of incredible power and what he said here ought to send shivers up our backs: This is how we will be treated if we do not forgive our brother or sister. That is the importance of forgiveness. The Greek word is *athame*, which means *to send away* -- Send away what separates us from other people. Send away our anger, our need for vengeance. If we want to taste divine life, we must discover forgiveness. The whole community brought together by Jesus is a *community of the forgiven ones.* Forgiveness is the key to knowing God.

We are never going to feel like forgiving our enemy. We must make a conscious, deliberate sacrificial choice of will in the name of Jesus to forgive our enemy. That is the true Christian work, the real Christian sacrifice. We do not need to fast. We do not need to get up at three in the morning to pray. We need to forgive.

The ancient fathers said, *"Picture this person that you cannot forgive, and say 'I bless you in the name of Jesus. Oh Lord, be blessed in that person.'"* This is how miracles are created. What happens when a person is forgiven? They have a chance at new life. We are no longer reducing them to what they have done to us. We are no longer reducing their identity to the wrong acts they have done. We are freeing them, seeing them for who they truly are and that is God-given grace.

All we need to do is to wish to be able to forgive and let the spirit of God come through us, causing a miracle happen in our lives and in the lives of the one that we forgive. Then all our wounds from the past will become treasures that generate compassion for others.

6

BELONGING:
THE PARABLE OF THE GOOD SHEPHERD
John 10: 1-30

'Very truly, I tell you, anyone who does not enter the sheepfold by the gate but climbs in by another way is a thief and a bandit. The one who enters by the gate is the shepherd of the sheep. The gatekeeper opens the gate for him, and the sheep hear his voice. He calls his own sheep by name and leads them out. When he has brought out all his own, he goes ahead of them, and the sheep follow him because they know his voice. They will not follow a stranger, but they will run from him because they do not know the voice of strangers.' Jesus used this figure of speech with them, but they did not understand what he was saying to them.

So again Jesus said to them, 'Very truly, I tell you, I am the gate for the sheep. All who came before me are thieves and bandits; but the sheep did not listen to them. I am the gate. Whoever enters by me will be saved, and will come in and go out and find pasture. The thief comes only to steal and kill and destroy. I came that they may have life, and have it abundantly.

'I am the good shepherd. The good shepherd lays down his life for the sheep. The hired hand, who is not the shepherd and does not own the sheep, sees the wolf coming and leaves the sheep and runs away—and the wolf snatches them and scatters them. The hired hand runs away because a hired hand does not care for the sheep. I am the good shepherd. I know my own and my own know me, just as the Father knows me and I know the Father. And I lay down my life for the sheep. I have other sheep that do not belong to this fold. I must bring them also, and they will listen to my voice. So there will be one flock, one shepherd. For this reason the Father loves me, because I lay down my life in order to take it up again. No one takes it from me, but I lay it down of my own accord. I have power to lay it down, and I have power to take it up again. I have received this command from my Father.'

Again the Jews were divided because of these words. Many of them were saying, 'He has a demon and is out of his mind. Why listen to him?' Others were saying, 'These are not the words of one who has a demon. Can a demon open the eyes of the blind?'

At that time the festival of the Dedication took place in Jerusalem. It was winter, and Jesus was walking in the temple, in the portico of Solomon. So the Jews gathered around him and said to him, 'How long will you keep us in suspense? If you are the Messiah, tell us plainly.' Jesus answered, 'I have told you, and you do not believe. The works that I do in my Father's name testify to me; but you do not believe, because you do not belong to my sheep. My sheep hear my voice. I know them, and they follow me. I give them eternal life, and they will never perish. No one will snatch them out of my hand. What my Father has given me is greater than all else, and no one can snatch it out of the Father's hand. The Father and I are one.'

We have here another teaching full to the brim with wisdom for daily living. Once again, we are dealing with spiritual metaphors that we need to unlock in order to discover what is inside of them. The parable takes place in the following context: Jesus has healed a blind man and the religious people come up to him and challenged his act of goodness. Just before this parable, we have Jesus saying, **"For judgment I have come into this world so that the blind will see and those who see will become blind,"** and the he further explains that by saying, **"If you are blind, you would not be guilty of sin but because you claim that you can see, your guilt remains."**

So the parable is a teaching on *spiritual sight*. The blind here are not literally blind people. They are all of us. We are them. We are the blind that Jesus has come to give sight to and in this seemingly simple scripture, we are given profound insight as to how we begin to see.

We are told that it was the time of the Festival of Dedication. This Festival is also known as Hanukkah and it commemorates the time in 165 B.C. when the Syrian King, Epiphanes, had taken over Jerusalem and placed in the Holy of Holies his own idol, *Baal Shalem*. The God announced by Moses as the one who is the core of Creation revealed through the Chosen People, had been removed for a pagan statue. Unclean animals like pigs were sacrificed in the very place where humanity had been given its first vision of Truth.

So Judas Maccabeus and his brothers revolted, overcame the Syrians and renewed the true worship in the Temple of Jerusalem. This is called the Festival of Lights. It is also known as *Renewal*. Jesus speaks to us right in time with the renewal of true worship. The theme here is spiritual blindness -- true worship. Hanukkah takes place in the winter time. Once again, we are in a spiritual symbolism that has to do with our heart of hearts. This is not about a season. This is about spiritual coldness, something all of us have tasted. Separation from God, walking in the winter of our hearts, no light, no understanding, no warmth, no joy, no peace. Who has not been down in that corner?

The whole point of Jesus' mission is to lift us out of that pit, to give us that light and warmth. This is salvation. That is wholeness of life. That is what the Creator wants for us. Each one of us has ended up in a winter spiritually and it is out of that winter that we must climb. This is not only about coldness of heart. There is an urgency here for each of us because, if we linger too long in the winter of our spirit, we become vulnerable to things of the dark, to the creatures of the dark, to the wolves out there in the dark. We become accessible to something other than God.

We can sink so low that we become instruments and victims of what lies in darkness and we must take seriously what Jesus is offering us because the alternative is devastation of our existence. Jesus says that the thief comes only to steal, kill and destroy. How many human lives are destroyed each and every day by that kind of spiritual darkness? So he shows us the path, the way out of that darkness, away from the wolves.

We are told in this teaching that Jesus is walking in the temple, in the midst of this renewal of worship time. That in itself has a meaning we need to understand. The temple that held the Presence of God according to the Tradition is being walked about in by Jesus who is the new temple. In this time of renewal of worship, Jesus is revealing that *he* is the temple of God, not those stones of Solomon.

It will eventually be revealed that, as we enter the way shown by Jesus, we become the temple of God. No human being could have imagined such a concept before the revelation of Jesus. They had to go to a "high place" to worship the mystery of reality which was so distant from them. Jesus brings it all home right down into our hearts. Jesus is the connection between human beings and God.

This is why he is "the unique one". This is not merely belief, nor a religion, but an encounter with the heart of God. We find him there in the temple, the temple itself in the flesh, among religious people for whom temples are made of stone and religion is outside of them. They surround him and say, **"How long will you keep us in suspense?"** The Greek is actually a slightly different translation: **"How long will you continue to annoy us?"** How long will you annoy us with this strange teaching? If we are honest with ourselves, we must consider how often we become annoyed with this God business. Jesus came to annoy us out of that winter of darkness in our heart of hearts.

They ask him: **"If you are the Messiah, tell us plainly."** This is the only time in the New Testament where Jesus is asked directly, *"Are you the messiah? Yes or no?"* And Jesus chooses not to give them a plain answer. Spiritual things have to be worked for. That is why our Maker has given us willpower. If a nine-foot angel of light appeared before us, it would be easy for us to be convinced about spiritual things. We would not have to do anything but be amazed. But it is more complicated than that. God wants us to use our will to make conscious decisions.

In order for us to love God, we have to make a choice. We have to change our ways. We have to want to get out of the darkness of selfishness where *we are* Baal Shalem, the idol in the temple. We have to get that idol out of our inner temple. So Jesus says: **"I have told you and you do not believe** and **the works that I have done in God's name, you have not believed."** For thousands of years, these chosen people, out of all the peoples of the earth, have been told by prophets and visionaries that the day was approaching when someone would appear and do these amazing things as a sign of God's presence in the world.

Yet even when people are healed miraculously, it is not good enough for them. Even when acts of compassion are done, they turn them against him. Unfortunately, "they" are us once again. We humans will take a good thing and find a spin on it to make it a bad thing. They could not accept the good that Jesus of Nazareth was doing and so their question to him is not that they want to know if he is the Messiah or not. They want to find a way to corner him, to get him.

It is the same with us. Do we really want to hear truth when we ask a question? Are we really seeking for something new or do we just want to hear what we already think we know? Those are the people who think they can see and who are condemned by their own unwillingness to recognize their blindness and let the teachings in. So Jesus says to them: **"My sheep know me."** The word sheep is a metaphor because in this season of Hanukkah, of renewal of worship, the quoted prophet of the time on the Sabbath before the celebration is Ezekiel. Ezekiel is one who talks about God as shepherd.

Unfortunately, we have turned the metaphor of sheep into a negative. In the seventies, when there was lots of talk about cults, the word "sheep" was used as a negative for people who just passively followed the guru. This is not at all what sheep means to Jesus when he talks about those who come after him. In the days of Moses, the sheep were the clean animals. For one thing, they were harmless. Children could approach sheep and not be bitten. Sheep had no way to defend themselves. They had no horns. They were not aggressive. They represented something of that wisdom from above, of which it is written: "**The wisdom from above is first pure then peaceable, gentle, willing to yield, full of mercy.**"

To be called "sheep" is not about being a passive doormat or a follower. To be a sheep according to Jesus is to be completely dependent on the shepherd, to have the courage to believe in God and God's goodness and Presence. That is courage, not passivity.

There are other metaphors that can get the point across to us. It takes an eagle to go the way of Jesus. It takes the lion of Judah to be the only one to choose mercy, to be the only one not to get into the gossip, to be the only one to stay positive in a world full of darkness. Let us not allow the metaphor of "sheep" fool us. It is about being strong and faithful enough to believe in God the Shepherd who leads us into green pastures. The shepherd must take the sheep to the place where they can eat. They cannot get there by themselves. They are completely dependent, just as we are, on the goodness of God.

The shepherd must also defend his sheep because they are made vulnerable by another characteristic: Sheep have a tendency to wander off. How often in one day do we disconnect with God? How often do we wander off from living in the way Jesus teaches us to live? When sheep are led into a gated area, they will find the one place that has a hole in it and wander off. We do that each and everyday in our hearts and need that shepherd to bring us back. This is why the metaphor of "sheep" is so appropriate.

Jesus says: "**My sheep, hear my voice.**" This is not about hearing voices. It refers to those who choose to go the way that he is showing: Mercy, forgiveness, kindness, not as a principle but in the moment when it is hardest to do. Jesus goes on to say: "**I am the good shepherd who lays down his life for his sheep.**"

Everyone knows the saying, *"Greater love has no one than he who lays down his life for those whom he loves"*. That saying has permeated our culture. Many people who know the saying, do not even know that it comes from Jesus. So they are missing a piece of the teaching. That word translated as *life* actually means soul. The soul is our desires and our thoughts and Jesus is teaching us that we must lose those former desires and thoughts that we had when we lived in the winter of our soul so that we might enter into a new way of life.

When we choose to sacrifice what we want for the sake of someone we love, when we choose not to have your requirements met for the sake of a higher love, we have entered the way of Christ. We have entered the transformation known as "laying down of our life."

We think of the loyal soldier who jumps on the grenade. That is not what this teaching means. We lay down our life, our soul, when we put our interests aside for others. When we do so, we find a new life, we enter into the spiritual life. It is not about being killed. It is about living abundantly. To "lose your soul for my sake" is to find new life. This is what Jesus means when he says, "**They hear my voice, they follow me.**" Consider the kind of sacrificial goodness it takes to choose someone else over ourselves in the name of God. This is how we are transformed and how the world is changed. This is the process of following Jesus.

And he says, "*To those who do this, who understand this teaching, I will give eternal life.*" Now, we tend to think of eternal life as a phenomenon experienced after we die. But that is not correct. The Hebrews did not think of eternal life as going from life to death and then dropping off into another dimension. Eternity is not a place. Eternity is a Presence. We read in John 17: "**And this is eternal life that they may know you, the only true God and Jesus Christ whom you have sent.**" Eternal life is experience of the Holy One, encounter with the depth of Spirit that never perishes.

So Jesus says, "**No one will snatch them out of my hand.**" He adds: "**What my Father has given me is greater than all else.**" What do you think he means? He is referring to you. You are God's gift to Jesus. You are greater than all else to Jesus. The purpose of the whole mission, of the Gospel is to save you out of darkness and fear and send you as sheep among wolves, unafraid because you are protected.

In that pen where the sheep are placed, there is a little opening which is where the wolves come in. The shepherd stands in that space. That is where God is in your life. Whenever you are afraid, whenever everything has fallen apart, remember that image. In that gap where darkness enters stands the good shepherd. This is why we say thank you.

7

DO NOT WORRY:
THE PARABLE OF THE LILLIES
Matthew 6: 26-34

Look at the birds of the air; they neither sow nor reap nor gather into barns, and yet your heavenly Father feeds them. Are you not of more value than they? And can any of you by worrying add a single hour to your span of life? And why do you worry about clothing? Consider the lilies of the field, how they grow; they neither toil nor spin, yet I tell you, even Solomon in all his glory was not clothed like one of these. But if God so clothes the grass of the field, which is alive today and tomorrow is thrown into the oven, will he not much more clothe you—you of little faith? Therefore do not worry, saying, "What will we eat?" or "What will we drink?" or "What will we wear?" For it is the Gentiles who strive for all these things; and indeed your heavenly Father knows that you need all these things. But strive first for the kingdom of God and his right-eousness, and all these things will be given to you as well.

'So do not worry about tomorrow, for tomorrow will bring worries of its own. Today's trouble is enough for today.

Most of us are familiar with this passage. We have all enjoyed its lovely, poetic expression. Perhaps some of us believe that it is a great saying of a first century hippie who had nothing to worry about. But that is certainly not the case. This is holy wisdom, eternal truth made known so that each of us might apply it to our lives. So we must consider this parable with the utmost seriousness.

One thing we all have in common is worrying and we take for granted that this is how things must be. Jesus gives us this teaching not as a platitude but as a specific instruction on how God wants us to live and he offers us the ways in which we must do it.

We will begin by taking a look at what this worry business is all about. There are certain things that make us worry, such as the evening news. Does a day go by when there isn't some kind of tragedy or frightening horror that occurs somewhere on this planet? When we pile on all of these awful news stories, they begin to build something up in us, some nameless fear that hangs over our psychology like a black cloud. What is the easy answer here? Turn off the endless stream of bad news.

Sometimes you have to choose where you put your attention in order to follow the teachings of Christ. You know that many of our young people spend hours and hours in front of a computer, playing games that are often violent. Something in you surely knows that this cannot be good. We have all seen news stories of young people imitating what they have been practicing all this time. Yet we blindly go on our way absorbing all of this negative imagery, poisoning ourselves and slowly but surely building this vast amount of unspecific fear and concern. And then suddenly, we hit the brick wall of the teachings of the Savior.

Worry is completely useless. If you are worried about the future, you actually don't know what is going to happen, you are just worried about it. You cannot do anything about it. You have suddenly mixed imagination with a few facts and created this condition of worry.

Here is one simple way of applying this life-transforming teaching. Next time you catch yourself worrying, ask the question, *"What can I do about this problem?"* If the answer is nothing, then stop worrying. Force yourself to stop worrying. When we spend so much of our energy in this condition of worry and anxiety, we are like a leaking cistern according to the prophet Jeremiah. We are just losing force on a daily basis. The strange thing about this bad habit that we all share is that it starts quietly in the morning and sneaks up on you, one little thing after another. Before you know it, it takes over the day and by evening, you are worn out. You've got a headache. You don't know why but it has not been such a good day.

Each day is the most precious thing we have. Jesus is practical. He wants us to use it well. He does not want us to waste years and years with something that is completely useless. If I had asked this question before the children left, "Does anybody not worry?" a few of them would have honestly raised their hands. That is why Jesus says we must become like little children. This is not idealism. It is down to earth, up close and personal. This is how you can live the way God wants you to live.

One of the things we need to know about worry is that it is an emotion. It is not a thought. Our mind is driven by this emotion that eats us up and has no logic. It does not help the problem. If you have got a problem and you are worried about it, worry makes it more difficult to see clearly and to solve your problem.

Emotions work 30,000 times faster than thought, according to some neuropsychologists. So we often have no control over this sudden influx of worry. Jesus came to set the captives free and we are the captives. One of the things we are captivated by is this constant dread, anxiety, and worry that we justify. Some of us actually enjoy it. Some of us worry about everything all the time. Each time an event comes up in our life, it is an opportunity to worry. You take worry away and some people have no more interests. Their hobby is gone.

That is deadly, physically and spiritually. When we allow ourselves to live any old way we want, not only does it affect our relation to God and to other people, but it comes right down to offending nature itself. If you are constantly churning, your blood pressure is going up, your organs are getting destroyed. The word worry in high old German is *wurgen* which means "choking". Worry and anxiety mean choking, straining, torment. That is no way to live.

Jesus came to set us free from the very things that eat us alive. First we have to be honest with ourselves. If we are the kind of person who gets a kick out of being worried, it is time to face up to our addiction. This is unhealthy living. Science has told us that when someone does an act of kindness towards another person, their level of serotonin goes up. Serotonin is used in anti-depressants to alter brain chemistry and make you feel better. If you are good to another person, it is proven that the other person's serotonin level goes up. Their immune system is strengthened and you have actually done some healing by an act of random kindness. Scientists tell us that our serotonin goes up as well in being good to another person. You heal yourself by living in a godly way.

If there is another person in the room watching this, their serotonin level goes up and that is how goodness is spread around the world, one person at a time. So everything matters, every little decision. Our problem is that we think of life as whatever is going on in the outside world when in fact our life is composed of our *reactions* to what is going on out there. It is inside, in our psychology, that we need to work by "cleansing the cup" as the Master says.

So we need to face the facts -- yes, I guess I do worry; yes, I just might enjoy it. Once we become honest with ourselves, then we can begin to apply this teaching. One of the things that causes us to worry, along with television and difficult things out there and bad habits, is everyone else around us. We are prisoners of worrying about what other people think about us. We are prisoners of, *"How dare they treat me that way? How can they speak like this to me? What are they thinking?"* How often does it turn out that this person who is looking at you with that nasty look on their face is not thinking about you at all while you are so tormented about it. Perhaps they just have indigestion.

Let me tell you a story someone sent to me. One Sunday morning, a mother went to wake up her son to go to church, entered his bedroom and said, "It's time to go to church." The son answered, "I'm not going today." The mother responded, "Why not?" The son says, "Two reasons. One, they don't like me. Two, they really don't like me." So the mother says, "I'm going to give you two reasons why you should go to church. Number one, you're 59 years old. And number two, you're the pastor!"

We are crippled by what we think other people are thinking of us. God wants us to be free. Jesus came to set the captives free, to set at liberty those who live in darkness. That is you and me. Darkness is worry, anxiety and anxiety at its root means double-minded.

In the letter of James, the apostle talks about being double-minded: **"If any of you is lacking in wisdom, ask God who gives to all generously and this is the wisdom we are here facing. But ask in faith never doubting for the one who doubts is like a wave of the**

sea driven and tossed by the wind for the doubter being double-minded and unstable in every way.”

He says that we *must not expect to receive anything from the Lord.* We must be united within regarding what is most important. Just before this statement you will notice a verse saying: **“No one can serve two masters. Either he will hate the one and love the other or be devoted to the one and despise the other.”** You cannot serve both God and, in this translation, money. The original is *mammon*, an ancient Aramaic word. Some suggest it is an ancient deity that represents material things -- not just cash but the way of the world.

So either we serve the Holy One, the spirit of goodness revealed by the Christ, or we serve the ways of this world where you get what you can, take care of number one and forget about the rest of it. This world is actively and aggressively pushing that agenda. It is its mindset and we need to choose which way we are going to go. If you are not following the agenda of the world in getting the latest electronic gadget and making sure that you have got what the neighbor has, then you suddenly cut down on your worry load a good deal and you start getting some free-dom and joy. The kingdom of God is – according to Romans 14's definition -- *peace and joy in the Holy Spirit.*

Worry is an emotion. When we start out the day, when we are getting our first cup of coffee and our orange juice, worry starts creeping in before we become aware of it. We *are* worry before we see worry. So one of the things we need to do according to our Teacher, is to

Watch and not sleep. Do no watch out there in the external world. Watch in here, in your psychology, in your soul. Next chance you get, when you are sitting at that breakfast table, take a look inside and see if there are any gremlins beginning to take over, to take you captive, to steal your joy and your peace and your right to be happy in this world.

One thing you may observe is that you are perhaps just sitting there with a big frown on your face. It is important to begin working with your body since emotions are so quick. If you become aware that you are frowning, just relax your brow. Release the tension in your body and you just might float up into happiness right then and there. This is your choice. Some people will actually choose, *"Thank you, I'll be miserable. My preference. It's a lifetime habit. It's the way it's supposed to be. I'm going to stick to it."* Good plan there. As the saying goes: How's that working for you?

Jesus is giving us a teaching to apply at our breakfast table so that God can get in and keep us from just wasting away. We all know emotions are hard to control. We are fragile creatures who must start in some way to deal with this thing called worry which ruins our lives. We cannot begin with emotions. We cannot control them so we have to start with the body. The very simple act of relaxing tension will free you from the captivity of this negative emotion of worry. This is not the kind of people God wants us to be even if we have behaved that way for a lifetime. There is another way.

Our commitment to Christ is to live that way, not to just stew in our juices until we drop dead. That is why it is called the "good news" because there is another option even if everything in us screams that "there's no way I can't worry". This is how you manage to overcome worry: *Jesus says not to and tells us how.* We have to use every way we can to follow his teaching. So you learn with the body to become aware of your tensions and you relax them and that releases you from a negativity you did not even know you had. Maybe you just had a bad dream. Maybe your feet were cold in bed or you're in a bad mood. Those little tiny things are what separate us from experiencing the presence of God in our daily life. That is why Jesus says that the kingdom of God is like finding a pearl of great price and selling everything just for that. His answer seems simple. It is one line. But because this is Holy Scripture, you can spend a lifetime on this one line.

Right before these words, he says, **"It is the Gentiles who strive for all these things."** That is the nice translation. Actually, the real word is *pagan*. It is the pagans who live like this, the godless ones who worry about this and that and everything else. But you and I have a shot at being at peace in spite of everything. How? **"Strive first for the kingdom of God and his righteousness."** We have all heard that one, no doubt. But it is a code word. The old word *kingdom* does not mean much to us nowadays. Consider this translation: *Put first in your priority the authority of God.*

If you believe there is a God, let God be present in your life by making room for God in your life. We shut God out by our fears, our tensions, our worries. And Jesus says to all humanity: *This is how you do this -- Focus on God and then you are free.* Slowly but surely, you are lifted out of the pit of a dreary life. It does not matter how old you are, how long you have done it. New life, new creation is available to each one of us all the way to our last day. We have the body and the mind over which we can have some control. We have a certain control over our thoughts so we can use those two things together to fight this enemy because to worry and to be anxious is to not trust God.

We also have our plans. We want to orchestrate the events of our life and we are worried about how they are going to come out. What is wrong with that picture? Where is God in it? Sometimes, what we have to do is learn to accept *what is*. That is a grown-up way. Accept what is. Not what you want, not what you've planned but what is and, as you do that, remember the name of God revealed to Moses: **"I am the One who Is."** You find God in what is, in the here and now. And we are never in the here and now because we want it to be something else that we have in mind. So we are always upset or worried over how things are working and never connecting with that which is reality, God, Spirit.

God has given us free will so that we can make the choice to trust God. We have to make that conscious effort to say: *"I'm not going to go this way. I'm going to go that way."* When you are at peace, when you let go of your requirements, you just might discover what this is all about. A great teacher, Karlfried Graf Durckheim, says: *Open the door and let yourself be found.* Open the door. Not a physical door -- your heart. Open and let spirit find you.

We have the door shut when we are uptight and stressed out and in a hurry and worried and anxious and that is why Jesus says you must be anxiety-free, not double-minded. Make first in your life the Presence of God, the teachings, the authority, the call and everything falls into place. Then all things work for good for those who love God. Even in the midst of illness, death, unemployment, if you hang on first and foremost to your trust in God, to your living as you are called to live according to the Savior.

So we can drop the worry habit. Leo Tolstoy, at age 50, suddenly had a revelation. He said that knowing God is like a child in his mother's arms. A little infant does not know who is holding him. He does not have a name for the person caring for them. But the child knows he or she is being held by someone who loves them. They are secure. They are content because somehow they know that those arms holding them are going to take care of them. That is the Gospel, the good news revealed by Jesus to us. So be free, take a risk and face life differently. Do not react the same old way. Learn new ways. Learn to sing a new song.

PARABLE WISDOM

8

MERCY:
THE PARABLE OF THE GOOD SAMARITAN
Luke 10: 25-37

*Just then a lawyer stood up to test Jesus. 'Teacher,'
he said, 'what must I do to inherit eternal life?' He
said to him, 'What is written in the law? What do you
read there?' He answered, 'You shall love the Lord
your God with all your heart, and with all your soul,
and with all your strength, and with all your mind;
and your neighbor as yourself.' And he said to him,
'You have given the right answer; do this, and you
will live.'*

*But wanting to justify himself, he asked Jesus, 'And
who is my neighbor?' Jesus replied, 'A man was going down from Jerusalem to Jericho, and fell into the
hands of robbers, who stripped him, beat him, and
went away, leaving him half dead. Now by chance a
priest was going down that road; and when he saw
him, he passed by on the other side. So likewise a
Levite, when he came to the place and saw him,
passed by on the other side. But a Samaritan while
travelling came near him; and when he saw him, he
was moved with pity. He went to him and bandaged
his wounds, having poured oil and wine on them.*

Then he put him on his own animal, brought him to an inn, and took care of him. The next day he took out two denarii, gave them to the innkeeper, and said, "Take care of him; and when I come back, I will repay you whatever more you spend." Which of these three, do you think, was a neighbor to the man who fell into the hands of the robbers?' He said, 'The one who showed him mercy.' Jesus said to him, 'Go and do likewise.'

There are many ways to understand a story. Here we have the best known story in the New Testament and we assume that we understand its teaching. I challenge you to see it another way.

The Good Samaritan's story is a spiritual teaching from the Master himself, from the Revealer of what it means to live God's life here and now. This is not merely an example of doing good, though it may seem that way on the surface. But the surface is not where we want to be if we are looking for things of God.

Consider the context of the story. Jesus has just said in verse 21, **"I praise you Lord of heaven and earth because you have hidden these things from the wise and learned and revealed them to little children."** Jesus is not talking literally. He never does. He is talking about receiving the things of God with *openness and purity*, with no guile. In other words, unlike most of us, who receive things with suspicion, prejudices, hatred, and block out Spirit from being made known to us. Receiving the things of God in that state of mind, that state of consciousness referred to by Jesus is the context for this story. We are told prior to the parable that an expert in the Law comes to the Master. He knows his teachings and he wants to trick Jesus into revealing that he is wrong somehow and he says, **"Teacher, what must I do to inherit eternal life?"**

Here is another moment in which we need to go deeper. This is not about the hereafter. Most of us are not seriously concerned about life after death. We are concerned about today and tomorrow and paying the mortgage and going to the hospital and the things of this life. The words "inherit eternal life" are code words. Inherit means *receiving a promised thing.* Our Creator has revealed to us that there is something promised to us, something other than an unhappy life, than a life full of mistakes, than a life of bitterness and anger and frustration.

The whole message of the revelation is that you and I -- creatures created by God -- are called to discover a different kind of life, a life of spirit, God's life in this world, here and now. Not after we die, but now. This is the freedom of the children of God and the ability to live morning, noon and night in a state of peace, joy, forgiveness and mercy. That is eternal life here and now, the life of spirit in this world. This is what the Gospel is about, the good news about entering that life while we are still in the flesh. This is possible for us and this example shows us one way that it can happen.

So Jesus says to this expert in the law, "**What is written in the law?**" Most of you know these great *Shema* prayers spoken twice a day by the Hebrew people: "**You shall love the Lord your God with all your heart and mind and soul and strength.**" In other words, everything comes second to that. And Jesus says, "**You've given the right answer. Do this and you will live.**" We will live now fully, the way we were meant to live, liberated from all of the burdens that oppress us because people who hate their neighbor are themselves oppressed, are themselves shutting off what life ought to be for them. But knowing something and doing it are very different things. The lawyer knew. He knew the Law, had it all memorized, but could not do it. So he tries to trick Jesus again. He says, *"Okay, but who he is my neighbor? Who should I love? Who in particular?"*

Then we have the story. A man was going down from Jerusalem to Jericho. If any of you have been on that road, it is a very strange road. It goes from 5000 feet above sea level to 1200 below in just 45 miles. It is rocky terrain, a perfect place for bandits of all sorts to assault the pilgrims on their way to Jerusalem. It is a dangerous road. In other words, that road from Jericho to Jerusalem is your road, my road, the road of life, full of hardship and obstacles, dangers, uncertainties. And sure enough, a man is attacked, beaten and left for dead, a bloody mess on the side of the road.

A priest goes by and we are told that he *passes on to the other side.* Now, most of us would assume, "Oh, what a bad guy." But Jesus is telling us something else. He is talking

68

about the best people who are walking to the other side because, in their world, if the priest went to a body and touched it, he would be contaminated according to their sacred laws and disqualified from his work in the temple. Or he might go over there and find out that it is a trick, a set-up for the robbers to catch him. So Jesus is not giving us examples of people who are not loving their neighbor. He is saying: *These are the good people who passed to the other side for good reason.* They have duties. They have obligations. Then he tells us that a Samaritan is coming along. You may know that there was a problem between Jews and Samaritans. Let me give you the details because this is where the story turns on its head and becomes very different in its meaning.

Seven hundred years before Christ, the Assyrians conquered that part of Israel, removed most of the Jews, leaving only a few and then filled the land with foreigners and Assyrians. The leftover Jews inter-married and created a new ethnic group that became known as the Samaritans. They changed the religion of the Jews, that sacred religion handed down from Moses to the Chosen People. They held to the first five books of the Torah and rejected all the rest. Not only that, but their temple was not in Jerusalem. It was on Mount Guerizon. The Samaritans had their own sacred place. In other words, to the Jews, they were the worst – worse than pagans -- violators of their religion, betrayers. This is the man who comes down the road in this parable.

You would have to be Jew and Palestinian to understand the degree of animosity between these people. This level of hatred had increased just fifty years before Christ. Pilgrims going to Jerusalem had been attacked by Samaritans and killed so Judeans came over and laid waste a number of villages. It could not be a more intense time of hatred between these two groups. Yet here we find that Jesus makes this man the hero of the story. In doing so, he turns it all around because the listeners who heard the words coming out of the mouth of Jesus could not see themselves in the role of the Samaritans, a hated half-breed who had desecrated their religion.

This story puts us in the role of the half-dead person on the side of the road, not the role of the Samaritan. This is not a story of doing good. This is a story of each of us, recognizing our desperate need for mercy, recognizing that we are half-dead on the side of the road. If we wish to live the life of God, to access the life of spirit, the question is: *"Will you allow yourself to be helped by your worst enemy?"* Will you in your need and weakness let a hated person whose name you cannot even say be the instrument of God's grace in your life?

Notice that Jesus asks the lawyer, **"Which of these three do you think was a neighbor to the man?"** And the lawyer says, **"The one who showed him mercy."** He cannot even say the word "Samaritan". That is how much they hate those people. They have shut off the possibility that God could do good through their enemy. We are called here to recognize our need, our condition and that we do not have the luxury of saying, *"I'll let that person help me but not that one. I don't like that one."* Our self-love cuts us off from being able to love our neighbor.

We hear the words "love your neighbor" and think, "I can be nice to the guy next door." What about the person whose name you cannot even mention without gritting your teeth? That is the Samaritan in your life. That is the impossible, accepting that person and then worse, *accepting help* from that person. This is the teaching embedded in the story of the Good Samaritan.

Self-love is not able to love in that way. This is why we must first love God with all our heart, mind and soul because it is out of a higher love that we can then manage to love another. Self-love has built walls around us. We have all heard of those images of hell as a lake of fire, but in reality, hell is self-love.

Hell is that love of self that cuts you off from being able to give or receive mercy, from being able to forgive. It is the hard work, the uphill work of going against our self-interest to the point where we permit the Samaritan to be the helper in our life. Consider how pride must bend! Think of the walls that must come down to get to that point. We need to recognize our state, our weakness, our vulnerability and to say: "*I need God's grace. And if it comes through my worst enemy, I will be thankful!*"

The final point of the story is that you never know in the Kingdom of God from where and through whom God is going to come to you to take those walls down. You don not want to miss that moment when Spirit reaches out to you through the most unlikely source and saves you from yourself, bringing you to new life.

9

ABIDE:
THE PARABLE OF THE VINE
John 15: 1-8

'I am the true vine, and my Father is the vine-grower. He removes every branch in me that bears no fruit. Every branch that bears fruit he prunes to make it bear more fruit. You have already been cleansed by the word that I have spoken to you. Abide in me as I abide in you. Just as the branch cannot bear fruit by itself unless it abides in the vine, neither can you unless you abide in me. I am the vine, you are the branches. Those who abide in me and I in them bear much fruit, because apart from me you can do nothing. Whoever does not abide in me is thrown away like a branch and withers; such branches are gathered, thrown into the fire, and burned. If you abide in me, and my words abide in you, ask for whatever you wish, and it will be done for you. My Father is glorified by this, that you bear much fruit and become my disciples.

We have before us one of the great teachings of the Christ. If you can only learn what is in this bit of scripture, your life might be completely different. You can have access to the power of Spirit from this scripture

alone. It is a mighty one and it begins from the very beginning when Jesus says, "**I am the true vine.**"

In the Gospel of John Jesus says "**I am the bread of the
world. I am the light of the world. I am the way, the
truth and the life. I am the resurrection and the life.**"
In this teaching, we have the last of the "*I am*" sayings: "**I
am the true vine.**" Because this is Holy Scripture, we
have to let it resonate deep within because that "I am" is
the same "*Ego Emi*" in Greek, the same "I am" from Ex-
odus chapter three verse 14 when Moses says, "**What
shall I call you? Who shall I say sends me back to
the Israelites?**" The answer from the Uncreated: "**Tell
them I am the One Who Is, I of timeless being.**" In
those two words, Jesus reveals his nature. From the very
beginning, the "Followers of the Way" understood that
out of that inconceivable core of the universe, out of that
higher intelligence that we cannot grasp, came the consciousness of the one we call Jesus the Anointed One.

In the Book of Revelation, we are told that we must be
either "hot or cold." Please do not be in the middle or "**I
will vomit you out of my mouth,**" says the Lord. So
this is our chance to make that choice once again. This is
a Truth we must revisit and seek to understand anew on a
regular basis.

Israel, the Chosen People, the ones who reveal to humanity the oneness of God, had a symbol for its identity:
The vine. In the Maccabean period, Jewish coins were
illustrated with a vine. In the days of Jesus, the temple of
Herod had a huge filigree vine that represented Israel. We

hear from the prophet Isaiah these words: **"For the vineyard of the Lord of hosts is the house of Israel."** Then soon thereafter we hear from the prophet Jeremiah: **" I planted you as a choice of vine from the purest stock. How then did you degenerate and become a wild vine?"**

When Jesus says, **"I am the true vine,"** it means that there is a also a *false* vine. Jesus is the new Israel. The word "Israel" means *God saves, God contends, God strives.* The name Jesus, *Yeshua*, also means God saves.

In the second verse today, we read that God prunes the good branches which are bearing fruit. Consider this statement very simply. A barren branch steals all of the energy, all of the nutrition that is meant for the fruit. If the vine grower is not constantly pruning, it grows wild at the expense of the fruit. We are the branches connected to the vine. We are meant to produce fruit and all of us without exception are in need of pruning. This is a lesson from the Christ saying that God prunes pride, impatience, unforgiveness, selfishness out of our life.

Consider a real situation in your life today where you feel the pain of such pruning. You have a choice to simply suffer and be bitter about it or to realize that you are being helped through the pain, that God is teaching you through what must be endured. We are being told by the Christ that if we were not being pruned, we would be nothing but a barren branch. What happens to these barren braches? They get cut off. They wither and they are burned.

The word "wither" is very appropriate here. How many lives do we see withering because they are not connected to the vine, to the power of God? Jesus says again and again, "**Abide in me.**" In other words: Realize that you have to be rooted in spirit, in God. What does it mean to be rooted? What does it mean to have such relationship, such a spiritual condition that you have access to that energy of the spirit? We have to understand the metaphor. What is this fruit that we grow to the glory of God? Each one of us is this fruit!

Think of all the meaningless pursuits and wastes of energy that consume our time. Think of the relationships that are toxic. Remember that these barren branches steal the energy from the fruit. So they must be removed from our lives or there will be no fruit. The Letter to the Hebrews, Chapter 12, tells us: "**Those whom God loves, God disciplines.**" To be disciplined is not to be punished, but to be taught. We have the opportunity to be the only people in the world who can use pain for good instead of just pain for pain. Every situation that you experience can be a teaching moment for you if you abide in Christ.

In Matthew, the word "abide" is found three times. It is found twice in Mark and seven times in Luke. In the Gospel of John, known as the "spiritual gospel," it is found forty-three times. We are urged to dwell, to live in, to stay with, to remain, to be connected to in order to produce fruit. If we do not, we wither. We are "**thrown into the fire.**" To be burned means that your life comes to nothing. You leave behind no legacy of meaning to anyone. You have come and gone. You have not done anyone any good, so nothingness is the future. The Savior is here precisely to save us from nothingness so that we can bear fruit to the glory of God.

What is the fruit? Christ-likeness, becoming like Christ. Galatians 5:22 tells us specifically about *love, joy, peace, kindness, generosity, faithfulness, gentleness, self-control* -- all of these fruits of the Spirit that God seeks to build within us so that we can be a good branch on the vine of Christ. This is unlike old Israel which deviated from that faithfulness according to the prophets and lost its way. With that descent comes judgment, not because God is an angry God, but because there are consequences to how we choose to live.

You might wonder why certain people behave the way they do. It is no longer because they are simply a barren branch with no love, with no Christ-likeness. It is because they have disconnected themselves from the source of spiritual power, spiritual healing, spiritual joy. You will notice that this passage does not say how to get onto the vine. It starts with us on the vine so this is a passage especially for those who seek to be Christians. You are already on the vine. You are already *cleansed by my word*, Jesus says, meaning that you have learned from Christ's teaching how to live as part of God's vine.

If you look at the great chapters 13 and 14 prior to this in the Gospel of John, you hear Jesus saying: "**If you love me, you will obey me.**" Then in chapter 14, he gives us this commandment: **"Love one another as I have loved you."**

That kind of love is not about feelings. It is not the love you hear on the radio, because we all know that love comes and goes. This is something else. This is *abiding in the vine*. This is a determination of the will to do what God calls us to do. We are told that we are either going to be tossed away or we are going to be pruned. As one minister put it: *"You're pruned if you do. You're pruned if you don't."*

One way or the other, we are going to be pruned. So those of us who delight in the Lord, who believe in something greater than ourselves, can let ourselves be joyfully pruned because we know that it enables us to evolve into a deeper connection with the vine. If you endure, if you suffer willingly, you bear more fruit. If you are willing to be patient in one situation, it gives you the power to grow in peace and forgiveness. This is cosmic math. It works.

Jesus says that **"if you abide in me, ask anything you want of the father and it will be done for you."** There is a form of prayer that does not include asking for all the different needs that God knows we have already. What does Jesus mean when he says such a thing? It reveals to us that when you get to that point of connection with Spirit, you are one with Jesus in saying – **"Your will be done."**

If you come to the point where you just want to do God's will, then that which you want is that which God wants and this is why you have answered prayers. It all comes back to one thing, which is being *connected to the source*. Otherwise, you are cutting yourself off from the very source of life, severing yourself from that which can be there for you when you need it.

We are not by ourselves. We are part of a vine. In this universe, we are all connected. We cannot be on our own, all alone. The barren branches, which bear no fruit of love and goodness, are incapable of manifesting the fruits of the Spirit without connection to God.

We do no have the power in ourselves to live in the way God wants us to live. We have to continually go back to that deeper source which feeds us in every way. Do you know that the barren fruit in Greek, that word *ferein* translated as "to bear much fruit" means *to endure hardship, to suffer willingly*. We have to walk into that cold wind, to accept what life throws at us and to see it from the perspective of God pruning us. That is another wonderful Greek word -- pruning. It has more than one meaning. It also translates as *cleansing*. He cleanses us of all the wrong and misused energy that makes us barren branches which can only be burned because they are of no use to ourselves, to the community, to the world.

Jesus put it very simply: "*I am the vine. Without me, you can nothing. I'm here to feed you, to help you bear fruit and whenever you're hurt, whenever things go wrong, you can even bear more fruit if you look at it right.*" First, we have to abide in Christ, then out of that comes all the fruit. Do not try to make up the fruit yourself, saying, "Hey look, I'm a good Christian. I've got some fruit here." You can go feed the hungry and still hate your neighbor. If you abide in Christ, then all things come out of the right place. Let that relationship, that dependence be at the heart of who you are because apart from that, we can do nothing.

Our destiny, our fruitfulness, is entirely dependent on the vine and our connection to it. Each of us is invited to this. Each of us is called to it. This is the spiritual power and joy that is offered to us each and every day if we make that one choice to abide, to dwell in the consciousness of Christ's reality, the center of our being.

10

BEING FOUND:
THE PARABLE OF THE LOST SHEEP AND THE LOST COIN
Luke 15: 1-10

Now all the tax-collectors and sinners were coming near to listen to him. And the Pharisees and the scribes were grumbling and saying, 'This fellow welcomes sinners and eats with them.' So he told them this parable: 'Which one of you, having a hundred sheep and losing one of them, does not leave the ninety-nine in the wilderness and go after the one that is lost until he finds it? When he has found it, he lays it on his shoulders and rejoices. And when he comes home, he calls together his friends and neighbours, saying to them, "Rejoice with me, for I have found my sheep that was lost." Just so, I tell you, there will be more joy in heaven over one sinner who repents than over ninety-nine righteous people who need no repentance.

'Or what woman having ten silver coins, if she loses one of them, does not light a lamp, sweep the house, and search carefully until she finds it? When she has found it, she calls together her friends and neigh-

bors, saying, "Rejoice with me, for I have found the coin that I had lost." Just so, I tell you, there is joy in the presence of the angels of God over one sinner who repents.'

These are parables that we all know, little stories filled with lovely pictures. Yet this is the holy power of God revealed to us, a massive revelation to humanity and to each one of us in particular. This is not a simple story. This is not a coloring book. This is Holy Scripture, divine wisdom for us today, the very heart of Christ's revelation of the mystery of God.

In order to decode this revelation, we have to understand the terms that have down through time taken on a meaning of their own and become encrusted with associations, assumptions, and prejudices that block out the light of what this is saying to us personally. Consider that word we find several times in the scripture, the word "*sinner*".

We do not like that word anymore. It is not politically correct. In fact, it makes us think of doing wrong, of guilt and shame that shrivel us up and make us think of original sin. But "original sin" is not biblical. The idea comes from St. Augustine, the most influential father of the western church for a thousand years. I prefer the term used by Matthew Fox: *original blessing.*

We have these ideas that we must overcome no matter how long we have carried them in order to see the living truth within them. The Greek word for sin is "*hamartano*" which means *missing the mark* like the archer shooting the bull's eye, missing the purpose, the direction of our life.

That mark that we are called to live out as children of God disappears very early in life. We get wounded. We get confused. We accept what others are telling us about ourselves. Before you know it, that glorious purpose of ours, that wonder of being alive in this universe is reduced to the old "death and taxes" or some silly notion that has no God in it, no holiness, no joy.

So here in one fell swoop, this simple parable comes to wake us up and lift us out of that illusory thinking. We find the term "**a sinner who repents**." Repent is another one of those words so caked with misunderstanding that we have basically thrown it out, we shut our mind to it. But repent comes from the Greek *"metanoia"*. It was translated in Latin to *"repentare"* in the early days.

Consider this word *metanoia*: *Meta* gives us metamorphosis; *noia* is the inner mind. Therefore the word translates as *transformation of mind*, transformation of how we see the world, transformation of attitude. It is no longer guilt and shame and that grim burden that has passed for religion for so long. We are told that whoever awakens to their true purpose in life makes God happy. You can cause Spirit to rejoice, just by awakening to who you truly are, by turning around and living your life in the Presence of God.

Then Jesus takes us into this wonderful story about the shepherd. God has been compared to a shepherd for centuries. In Ezekiel chapter 34, we read: "**I will seek for**

you as a shepherd on a dark and cloudy day. I will seek the lost." From the beginning, this has all been about God seeking the lost. That is the heart of the matter. The irony is that *we* are the lost and we do not know it. This good shepherd, this God image incarnated in a story line, leaves aside all his beloved sheep to go find the lost one.

Consider this: Would the average shepherd sacrifice the ninety-nine to get the one? How is that going to work at the market place? This is not good business. So what does this mean? He goes in search of the one lamb. Notice that he did not pick a different animal for this parable. Why is that? Dogs tend to run off. Sheep are different. They do not want to go away. They just wander around, get some grass here, then move over there and before they know it, they are lost. The flock is gone. They cannot find their way home. And what happens to a sheep that is lost? It panics. It runs in circles and becomes easy prey to the wolves, easy prey to the forces of darkness. It is risky business being a lost sheep. And who among us has not been lost? Who among us has not been prey to feelings of despair, abandonment, hopelessness? It is the human condition.

We are all the lost lamb. We are all in need of being found by God. We are all in need of coming home. What does it mean to come home? To awaken to God, to that reality that can transcend all our issues, even death itself.

It is possible to find that peace in the midst of this uncertain world. It is possible to come home to your spiritual center, but the real revelation in this parable is about the nature of God. God is revealed as leaving everything to find you, to find the lost lamb. What kind of love is that? This is a seeking God. Some of us do not even want to be found. Some of us get found in spite of ourselves. Some of us do not know that we are lost. But the God revealed by Christ is always trying to call us into our true purpose, our true self, our true belonging.

Now the Pharisees are standing there muttering and criticizing because the holy man is speaking with sinners and tax collectors who have come to him. They know that something is different about this rabbi. Unlike the Pharisees who are full of self-righteousness and look down on them, Jesus is searching for them to bring out their true nature out and to make them pleasing in the sight of God.

In the original Greek, the ninety-nine righteous ones are not those "who have no need of repentance". The accurate translation reads *"those who do not believe they have any need of repentance."* As long as you do not feel that you need anything, you cannot be found. You are more lost than the rest. We are all in need of being found by God and not just one time, but again and again. We are constantly in danger as these sheep-like creatures who wander off by mistake, who wake up one morning and find that we have made a terrible mistake and cannot find our way home.

The metaphorical revelation of God's nature as "the good shepherd" is often pictured as a figure who puts the lost lamb on his shoulders. In other words, the strength of God carries us home. The power of Spirit, goodness itself will pick you up and bring you back! You do not have to do it by yourself. You do not have to depend on your limitations and brokenness to limp home. You will be carried on the shoulders of the One who is love itself. God is not only looking for you. God will lift you up and bring you home.

There is yet another dimension to this parable. If God is always seeking the lost, then those who are followers of the way, as Christians were first called, must also be seeking the lost. Our spiritual obligation is to seek the lost who need to be found, who need to recognize that they are spiritual beings who are called to be happy in this world and conscious of the Presence of God.

Consider now that other parable of the woman and the lost coin. This is not about a miserly woman who needs to find her money. Jesus mentions ten silver coins, which is exactly what is in the headdress of Mid-eastern women of the past. It was their dowry, their identity, their gift to their marriage. By sacred law, it could not be taken from them. So these ten silver coins were more precious than any other possession.

We have in this parable a methodology for inward searching. We have to seek what we have lost within. Have you seen what life has done to you? Have you seen how it has hardened your heart, how you have put up walls, how you lose your humanity so easily? The widow reminds us of what we are to do to regain that which is most precious in the following three steps.

1) She recognizes that she is in darkness and must turn a light on to find what has been lost. What is that light? It is knowledge. It is the teaching. It is recognizing the Presence of God among us. And then what does she do?

2) She sweeps the floor. In those days, it was made of hardened mud and covered with hay. She must sweep the floor bare. She must sweep bare her situation. She must be honest about her condition. We have to lay bare the truth of our life.

3) Thirdly, she searches diligently. Nothing is more important than to find it. Nothing is more important than for you to find your spiritual self, that kernel of the divine within you, that connection with God. Having found it again, you partake in the joy of the Master, the joy of God toward you, the lost sinner, who has come home. That is our journey and our salvation.

11

SPIRITUAL SIGHT
HEALINGS AS PARABLE
Mark 10: 46-52

They came to Jericho. As he and his disciples and a large crowd were leaving Jericho, Bartimaeus son of Timaeus, a blind beggar, was sitting by the roadside. When he heard that it was Jesus of Nazareth, he began to shout out and say, 'Jesus, Son of David, have mercy on me!' Many sternly ordered him to be quiet, but he cried out even more loudly, 'Son of David, have mercy on me!' Jesus stood still and said, 'Call him here.' And they called the blind man, saying to him, 'Take heart; get up, he is calling you.' So throwing off his cloak, he sprang up and came to Jesus. Then Jesus said to him, 'What do you want me to do for you?' The blind man said to him, 'My teacher, let me see again.' Jesus said to him, 'Go; your faith has made you well.' Immediately he regained his sight and followed him on the way.

Embedded in these words is a teaching, a divine revelation, a set of instructions for each of us. So be sure that this is not about some old blind man in the first century. It is about each of us right here, right now. That is what makes these words Holy Scripture.

89

We are told that Jesus is on his way and comes upon this blind man by the side of the road. Another translation reads that the blind man is "alongside the way." On the way that Christ is walking, along the side of it is the blind man.

It is the only time in the Gospel of Mark that we have a name mentioned in the healing stories. You know that the gospel writers did not merely write something to the effect that "Joe was sitting over there one day." There is a teaching here. It is found in the name Bartimaeus. *Bar* means "son of," as in *Yeshua bar Joseph*, Jesus son of Joseph. Here we have Bartimaeus, son of Timaeus, and Timaeus means "the Worthy One." The blind man is the son, the child of the Worthy One. Now who might that be, do you think?

It is you and me. We are all children of the Worthy One, are we not? So this is about our blindness, our spiritual blindness, our need to reach out to the healing love of God.

One of the ancient disciplines is *lectio divina* where we study scripture prayerfully and very slowly because there is so much in it. Consider the use of this metaphor of the blind man, One thousand years before Christ, in the Book of Leviticus, we find a sacred law that says, "**No one who has a blemish, blind or lame, shall draw near to my sanctuary, shall profane my sanctuary.**" In primitive times, it was believed that to be crippled in some way or other, to be imperfect was an evil impurity that had no place in the sanctuary.

The prophets came along to announce a change in the understanding of these teachings. Isaiah proclaimed: "**I will lead the blind by ways they have not known. Along unfamiliar paths, I will guide them. I will turn the darkness into light before them and make the rough places smooth.**" That revelation coming through the old prophet finds fulfillment in this story five hundred years later.

In this little parable, in this few verses, we are shown the way in which a blind person begins to see spiritually, the way in which we connect with Spirit. We find that the blind man -- you and me -- begins to shout. That is a teaching right there. He begins to shout, "**Son of David, have mercy on me!**" Here is the beginning of the invocation of the Holy Name, also known as the "Jesus Prayer" of Eastern Orthodoxy: "*Lord Jesus Christ, Son of God, have mercy on me, a sinner.*" This is one of the earliest methods of Christianity invoking the power of the Holy into our situation. When we cry out, we find response. As it is written in Psalm 34, "**I sought the Lord and he answered me.**"

From the beginning of the biblical revelation, we are told there is a response for those who seek. Dare to call upon the mercy of God. What happens then? In this teaching, we are told: *Many rebuked him.* This man runs into obstacles while calling upon the mercy of God.

How many of us dare not speak our faith in public? How many of us know that the invocation of the name Jesus in our culture is most often as a curse word, not as an invocation of the Holy? There are obstacles in our way. There are people who make us feel ashamed to be believers. But worse yet, there are voices within us that are obstacles to our reaching out to God. There are parts of us that are full of doubt and cynicism, that want to do it alone, that do not want to be that vulnerable. It takes vulnerability to say, "Have mercy on me." That is when the door opens.

A philosopher once said: *"Open the door and let yourself be found."* Most of us hide behind closed doors emotionally and spiritually. There are obstacles to that simple thing of calling out to God. Pride is in the way. So what does the teaching tell us? **"He shouted all the more."** He shouts all the more in the face of obstacles. What does that teaching mean? *Perseverance!*

It is necessary to persevere and then to persevere some more. All these stories of faith tell us that we must persevere. Never give up. Keep trying. Do not let the voices within or without stop you from connecting with God's mercy.

What do we read next? Jesus is walking along the way and suddenly – **"Jesus stood still."** Jesus stands still and looks at you. When you call out to Christ for mercy, Jesus will turn and listen to you. **"Call him,"** he says. So they called the blind man and say, **"Cheer up."** This is a poor translation. The word is *tarse*, a term that we find seven times in the New Testament, six of them on the lips of

Jesus. It means: *take heed, be of good courage, be strong.* We find it first in the prophecies of Zephaniah: "**On that day it shall be said to Jerusalem -- *Tarse*. Do not fear, it means. Do not fear, oh, Zion. Do not let your hands grow weak. The Lord your God is in your midst, a warrior who gives victory**." That is the meaning at the heart of that word: *Take courage. Do not fear..*

Then comes the next teaching. This is where lectio divina is critical. You can be reading along and miss a divine teaching: "**Throwing off his cloak…**" This beggar blind man has one thing in life to keep him warm, to keep him comfortable, to protect him from wild dogs, from the stones of those passing by and that is his coat. It is his whole life. It is his *old life* that he must throw off in response to the Holy One.

The instruction is: If you want to go to the Holy, you have to throw off the old -- the old attitudes, the old personalities, the old belief systems. That is our smelly coat, ragged and yet so familiar. Some of us will choose to stay under that coat by the side of the road and die there. The teaching today tells us to throw it off!

The next teaching is: "**He jumped up.**" He did not say, "*Well, maybe tomorrow, I can talk to him.*" This is the disease of tomorrow, from which we all suffer. The teaching is that he jumped up.

We are promised that there is response to our calling out with perseverance. But once the response comes, what are we to do? We are to throw off the old ideas of ourselves, our ideas of God, and jump up in response. Then the Holy One asks us: **"What do you want me to do for you?"**

After a lifetime of seeking, stumbling, failing, we finally connect with Spirit and the question is: *"What do you want me to do for you?"* We have to know what we need. This is not the time to say, *"I think I would like a Mercedes, please."* We have to be tuned in to our need enough to be ready for the question. Now that we have finally tuned in to Spirit, what is it that we want from Spirit after all? What is it that you need from God now? Surely, it is to have a fuller life, to be your deeper self, to find your destiny.

The blind man says it for every one of us: **"Teacher, I want to see."** I want to perceive you in all things. I want to see Reality as it is. I want to know you. I want to taste and see how good you are.

You can take a quantum leap into that seeing by simply dropping everything else in your head, in your heart and seeing the glory all around you. That is one small way to connect with the Eternal. So Jesus says: **"Go. Your faith has healed you."** How has faith healed him? How has faith given him the ability to see? How has the miracle taken place? Perseverance, knowing our need in our condition, daring to be vulnerable enough to say, *"I need help, Lord. Help me."* Dare to trust in the Holy One, to cry out to him and, once you get his attention, cry out the greatest need of your spirit, *"Lord, help me to see. Help me to know you that I may taste and see how good you are."*

Then what happens? Immediately, Bartimaeus **"gets on the way."** He *follows on the way*. He becomes part of that way of life which is the Christ way, leaving that old, smelly coat behind.

PARABLE WISDOM

12

FROM THE HEART:
THE PARABLE OF THE BLIND LEADERS
Matthew 15: 10-14

Then he called the crowd to him and said to them, 'Listen and understand: it is not what goes into the mouth that defiles a person, but it is what comes out of the mouth that defiles.' Then the disciples approached and said to him, 'Do you know that the Pharisees took offence when they heard what you said?' He answered, 'Every plant that my heavenly Father has not planted will be uprooted. Let them alone; they are blind guides of the blind. And if one blind person guides another, both will fall into a pit.'

The Pharisees had asked Jesus, "**Why do your disciples not wash their hands before they eat?**" There is no place in the Old Testament that says you must wash your hands before you eat. This was a ceremonial ritual which the priests had to perform according to the law of Moses to go into the Holy of Holies in the temple. The Pharisees knew that this man Jesus was a rabbi and that his people ought to behave like all the other followers of these commandments.

The Pharisees functioned as the religious police. Things must be done according to all the rules. Jesus responds to

97

all rigid rule keepers down through time: **"It is not what goes into your mouth that makes you unclean. It is what comes out of it."**

In this simple saying, Jesus has shocked the Pharisees and the Jewish people like no other saying in the New Testament. In one fell swoop, he wipes out entire sections of the Book of Leviticus, the dietary laws that made them the Chosen People of God. These are the Kosher laws which made them separate from all other people. They believed that they followed God's commandments by obeying these strict dietary laws. It was all about holiness, and holiness is about following the will of God.

The whole identity of the Chosen People was wrapped around these commandments related to eating. The carpenter from Nazareth throws it all out. So disciples come to him and say, **"You have offended the Pharisees."** What does Jesus do? He offends them some more. He says, **"Leave them alone. They are blind guides."**

We have abused these Pharisees for centuries but they were the most religious segment of the most religious people on earth. The Pharisees were the good guys. They were just thinking of holiness as *faithful observance of the rules.* In this saying, Jesus has changed the whole nature of religion. He has taken it away from an external set of rules to an internal requirement. His own disciples do not understand what he is talking about. They cannot believe it either because he is shredding everything they know. They ask: *"Explain this dark saying to us about what comes out of the mouth is unclean. We don't get it."* Jesus responds with typical blunt honesty: "**Are you so dull? Are you so without understanding yet as my disciples?**"

He says it to us as well as we try to understand this teaching. He tells us that what comes out of the mouth comes from the heart. The Hebrews did not merely consider the heart to be that organ which pumps blood. The heart is the *center of our being*. Jesus puts religion at the center of your being. He takes religion away from commandments about food and ceremonies and rituals and makes it about thoughts, feelings, motives, conscience.

Take something like anger. In today's pop psychology, we are often told: "*It's good to vent your anger. Just let it out. That will make you feel better.*" Jesus says: "**What comes out of your mouth makes you unclean.**" Jesus tells us that it is not just murdering your brother which is the commandment handed down from Mount Sinai. It is the thoughts of hatred and anger within you that are considered the sin of murder. He takes religion into places we do not want him to go, where no one sees us. That is where religion (meaning "re-linking with God") takes place.

Jesus quotes Isaiah saying, "**These people honor me with their lips but their hearts are far from me.**" The next verse is "**they worship me in vain.**" Another translation says *their worship is worthless.*

Jesus took religion from the observance of rules and regulations to the purposes that those rules and regulations are supposed to serve. He pointed to the spirit of the commandments. There are religious teachers among us today who still do not get it, who are the blind leading the blind and falling into a pit, a pit of judgment, hatred, separation. They have missed the spirit that Jesus came to reveal.

The teachings of Jesus are not simply Holy Scripture. They are about Jesus' *interpretation* of scripture. Jesus is the light that has come into the world so that we will not be blind anymore. Jesus' interpretation takes us right into spiritual things. In the Letter to Timothy, it is written: **"To the pure, all things are pure."**

That is religion. It is about who you are in the privacy of your life and the choices you make. The prophet Jeremiah tells us that God searches our hearts and minds and rewards according to our conduct. The reason religion has been such a disaster in the world, the reason why religion has burned people alive in the name of Jesus is because the blind people took over again and went after the rules and the regulations rather than the spirit.

I did a radio show once and someone called in asking, *"What's the difference between religion and spirituality?"* Many people are looking for God, for meaning in this age, but they do not want to come to church because religion has been a thing of condemnation to them. They want to find goodness and light and love so they go some place else. Religion has become institutions and rules instead of the spirit of Christ in your heart.

Jesus has made religion much easier and much more difficult. We do not have to follow all those rules that we find in the Old Testament. But we now must deal with that place deep within where we live and breathe, where we react to things, where we make choices, where we let ourselves get away with ugly behavior. That is the place where religion now takes place for those who follow Jesus. It is easy to obey a thousand rules every day and then to go and hate your neighbor. This is the story of humanity. But Jesus was a spiritual radical. His revelation was to bypass all the nonsense and connect us directly with God. In doing so, he broke all the rules and they crucified him for it. You just might get crucified for it as well if you choose the kind of spiritual freedom that he gives you.

The Bible is a map to the heart of God and the way we get there is by purifying our own heart. Even in the Old Testament, we hear the prophets beginning to speak of the way of Christ. Hosea says, *"I don't want your sacrifices. I want mercy. I want knowledge of God, not burnt offerings. I want your experience of the Holy."* Holiness is a purified heart.

That is a hard journey but it is the spiritual journey. It is the narrow way. So the next chance you get to react as you have always reacted, remember this: It is your opportunity to do it differently in the name of Christ. Then you just might get to taste and see how good the Lord is, and how real and present He is. This is the gift of Jesus to us in this teaching.

PARABLE WISDOM

13

A NEW CREATION:
THE PARABLE OF THE GRAIN OF WHEAT
John 12: 20-26

Now among those who went up to worship at the festival were some Greeks. They came to Philip, who was from Bethsaida in Galilee, and said to him, 'Sir, we wish to see Jesus.' Philip went and told Andrew; then Andrew and Philip went and told Jesus. Jesus answered them, 'The hour has come for the Son of Man to be glorified. Very truly, I tell you, unless a grain of wheat falls into the earth and dies, it remains just a single grain; but if it dies, it bears much fruit. Those who love their life lose it, and those who hate their life in this world will keep it for eternal life. Whoever serves me must follow me, and where I am, there will my servant be also. Whoever serves me, the Father will honor.

Sacred teaching has many levels and we cannot read it just on the surface. These are holy writings. The spirit of the Almighty inspired the great prophet Isaiah to write these words: **"I, the Lord, have called you in righteousness to open eyes that are blind, free captives from prison, release from the dungeon those who sit in darkness."**

Here we have the prophecy of the coming Messiah, announcing the appearance of Jesus in human history which would give us a way of understanding that would free the captives, open eyes of blind people, release people from dungeons. And why is this of interest to us? We are the blind. We are the captives. We are the ones who sit in darkness in the dungeons and it is for us that these scriptures are written.

Eight verses later in the same chapter of the same prophet, we read: "**I will lead the blind by ways they have not known. Along unfamiliar paths, I will guide them. I will turn darkness into light before them and make the rough places smooth.**" Do we not all have some rough places that need to be made smooth in our lives?

In the Book of Isaiah, chapter 35, the prophet has a great vision of the coming Messiah who will reveal us how to live, how to find meaning. The visionary describes this as "the desert will blossom." He is not talking about sand in the Middle East. He is talking about the desert of the human soul. He prophesizes: "**Then the blind, the eyes of the blind will see. The ears of the deaf will be unstopped. Then the lame will leap like a deer. The mute tongue will shout for joy. A highway will be there in this desert. It will be called the way of holiness. The unclean will not journey on it. It will be for those who walk on that way.**"

This is a clue, a code breaker. The way of holiness is a teaching that gets under your skin, into your daily life, deals with your business, with your secret places. This is not about social classes and all the good that we do as Christians. The revelation of the Messiah is to put you in touch with the Holy Spirit, to fill you with freedom from yourself. Each of us live in our own dungeon. Each of us is a victim of the wounds we have received in life. This is our captivity. The prophet was saying that the change would take place not in the outside world but within each of us. This is a map to self-change for our own well-being.

When Jesus came to Nazareth at the beginning of his ministry, he walked up the steps into the synagogue, opened the scroll to chapter 61 of Isaiah and read: "**The spirit of the Lord is upon me because he has anointed me to preach good news to the poor, to proclaim liberty to the captives, release from darkness for prisoners.**" This was a mission statement. But it has been misunderstood because several verses later, the prophet says that these captives, prisoners, blind, poor, these who encounter the spirit through the teachings of Christ, will be made *oaks of righteousness*. These great oak trees are rooted in God, and identified as "a planting of God for the display of His splendor."

There are people who display the splendor of God. They radiate goodness, self-transcendence, and forgiveness. This is freedom from captivity -- the captivity of our selfishness, of all the things that keep us locked in our dungeon. It is in this context that we hear this incredible saying of Christ. He has just come into Jerusalem and has been received with those palm leaves and branches that are so familiar. They were used in the days when Syrians ruled Jerusalem with an iron hand, burned the scriptures, tortured the priests, turned the temple into worship of idols. One Judas the Maccabean, or Judas the Hammer, rose up and his forces pushed out the Syrians. The grateful people raised palm branches at his arrival in Jerusalem, but then one hundred years later, the Romans took over and it was the same thing all over again.

So here comes Jesus and the people believe he is another liberator who is going to give them their political freedom. They raise those palm branches once again, but only to discover that he came for something else which they did not understand, and so they crucified him. He says, "**In truth I say to you.**" New Testament translations often have him say: "**Verily, I say to you.**" The exact translation from the Greek is: "**Amen, amen I say to you.**" Jesus is saying: "*Most solemnly I tell you an absolute truth from the depths of God,*" and here it is, this absolute truth that the Savior speaks to us – "**If a grain of wheat does not fall into the earth and die, it remains a single grain. But if it dies, it bears much fruit.**" What he describes here about dying is the process of transformation that puts us in touch with the Spirit, that leads us into a knowledge of the kingdom of God here in this time and place. We are grains of wheat sowed by the Holy One and if we do not go through this process described by Jesus -- giving ourselves up -- we bear no fruit, we end up all alone.

In Ephesians we read: "**Once, you were darkness but now, you are light in the Lord. Live as children of light. You are people belonging to God declaring the**

praises of him who called you out of darkness into his wonderful light." What is the darkness? What is light? Each of us knows deep in our hearts that there are places within that must change. The question is, do we want to change?

But you might ask, "*Why should I not behave in the old way I want? Just as it naturally comes? Just the way I am? Why should I not talk to people just the way I feel or deal with life and its incidents just the way it comes naturally?*" Freedom in God's world is the ability to do what is right. God has given us the capacity to do what is right but it doesn't just come naturally. We have to undergo a process, an effort.

There once was a man who found a cocoon with a little hole in it and a butterfly was trying to come out of it. He watched it for hours and the butterfly was having trouble coming out so he took a pair of scissors, snipped the cocoon, and let the butterfly out. But it came out all shriveled. Its wings were incomplete, it could never fly. The man did not realize that the struggle which the butterfly undergoes in the restricting cocoon is precisely what creates the wings and sends fluid into them so that he can fly. It is our struggles that make us strong. Our struggles give us the ability to fly spiritually.

But we take the easy road. Then Jesus tells us, "**Those who love their life will lose it. Those who hate their life in this world will gain into eternal life.**" Jesus brings us abundant life. This is not about hating life. The Greek words for "*he who loves his life will lose it*" actually mean "*he will devote it to destruction.*" If you live only for yourself any way you please, you devote your life to destruction and you become just one of those lonely grains of wheat buried in the ground.

When that seed breaks open in the ground, it is the interior design, what it is truly meant to be, that comes out. So it is your true self that Christ is trying to bring forth. See how dangerous it is to misunderstand these words. It is not about hating your life. It is about hating to live a barren, meaningless, pathetic life in a dark dungeon of self-interest. Jesus gives us the key to our liberation and each of us in our own way has our work cut out for us. That is why it is called the narrow way because most people want to do it the easy way.

No matter where you are in life, the teachings seek to tell you how to get on the way of renewal, what you have to face in yourself. Do that work, make that effort, die to your fears, your impatience, your pettiness and discover what is on the other side. Discover the new life: **"Whoever is in Christ is a new creation. The old has passed away."** People can become glorious children of light in this world and this is what salvation means.

So face those limitations, that old shell which locks you out of God's joy, which keeps you from being an instrument of goodness in this world. Let it die. Let it dissolve, let it break open and come out in the name of God into a life that is worth living, full of meaning, full of joy, full of miracles. God will use you when you come out of your dungeon and your darkness into his wonderful light.

14

FAITH:
THE PARABLE OF THE MUSTARD SEED
Luke 17: 5-10

The apostles said to the Lord, 'Increase our faith!'
The Lord replied, 'If you had faith the size of a mus-
tard seed, you could say to this mulberry tree, "Be
uprooted and planted in the sea", and it would obey
you. 'Who among you would say to your slave who
has just come in from ploughing or tending sheep in
the field, "Come here at once and take your place at
the table"? Would you not rather say to him, "Pre-
pare supper for me, put on your apron and serve me
while I eat and drink; later you may eat and drink"?
Do you thank the slave for doing what was com-
manded? So you also, when you have done all that
you were ordered to do, say, "We are worthless
slaves; we have done only what we ought to have
done!"'

Many of us have heard this scripture over and over again.
I am going to ask you to put aside your associations of
what you thought it meant and to try to hear it in a fresh
way. This is the living teaching of Jesus and it is a teaching about the nature of faith. Perhaps we think we know
what faith is. This teaching tells us we that we do not.

Let me put it in context for you. At the beginning of the reading, Jesus is telling us how we must live, what we must be like in order to live in God's Presence. We must go over the translation carefully because these are words going all the way back to the Aramaic which carried a stronger density of meaning than the English language. Jesus says, concerning certain behaviors, that it would be better to have a millstone placed around our neck. A millstone is a thousand pound rock that was used to crush grain. Jesus the Christ is telling us that it would feel better if we had a thousand pounds around our neck and were dumped in the ocean and sunk hopelessly to the bottom. That would be a better deal for us than what is going to be our fate if we cause others to stumble.

The "little ones" whom we might cause to stumble are not children. The Greek is *microi*. This is the word for those who are struggling to be faithful or "little in faith," those who are seeking to please God, those who are nothing other than each one of us. We are the little ones doing what we can, failing, trying again. We are the little ones trying to find our way back to God, sometimes in spite of ourselves, and Jesus is saying: *"Beware that you do no interfere with another human being's effort to reconnect with God."*

Just a little wrong behavior can cause tremendous damage to another soul. On a larger scale, there are many people who have had to leave churches and the Christian teachings because they were utterly crushed by bad theology and even worse, un-Christian behavior inside a church.

There are many people whom we might call "recovering Christians," people who were given such a twisted version of religion – full of judgment and condemnation – that they had to run away from Christianity to try to find God. Consider the responsibility of the ministers and of the congregations who fail to behave as Christians and cause these people to walk away from God forever.

What does that tell us? That in the smallest things and the smallest behavior, we are profoundly responsible. Most of us live any old way we want. We do not really care what breaks around us. If you believe in any of these teachings, Jesus is saying that you would be better off with a thousand pounds around your neck than behaving so recklessly and causing someone else to lose their chance to know God. That is quite a responsibility which we are stuck with it whether we like it or not.

The disciples ask Jesus: **"Increase our faith."** This is in response to the Master saying that we must forgive seventy times seven. That is a spiritual code from ancient Hebrew teaching.

The number seven had a very special meaning. It was the number of perfection. It represented the perfection of God as opposed to the number six which represents imperfection. This is why it is written that there were seven days of creation. Think of the madness of religion fighting science trying to prove a literal meaning to seven days. Rather, this is a symbolic expression of the beauty of God's work represented by the number seven.

Jesus is saying we have to forgive an infinite number beyond even the number of perfection. He teaches that, if the person comes back to you and repents, you must forgive. So it is not simply a blank check, but response to repentance.

We must be able to forgive someone as we are forgiven. Why is that? Because that is the manifestation of God's own mercy in the world. He reveals to us that the cosmic truth of the universe is that the measure with which we give is the measure with which we receive, even from God. We block the flow of God's mercy with our lack of mercy.

So Jesus says: *"Watch yourself. Pay attention to yourself. Guard yourself."* There is an ancient teaching in Christianity called *the watch of the heart* where you have an inner awareness of what is going on inside of you, of what thoughts and emotions are circulating within.

Most of us do not guard the heart at all. Any thought comes through, even murderous, horrific, demonic thoughts, thoughts that do not originate with us. They just come through us like a radio station but we do not pay any attention.

Jesus says to all of us: *"Pay attention not just out there but in here, especially in here."* That is the beginning of change. That is when the disciples say: *"Increase our faith, please."*

They are simply saying what you and I know in our hearts.

These are the disciples who gave up everything -- career, family, future. In fact, most of them gave up their lives to follow this holy man who is breaking all the rules. One would think that they would have some wisdom by now. But they know they do not have enough. They have enough to leave everything they know, yet they do not have enough to find release from inner attitudes.

What does Jesus say? **"If you had *any* faith..."** – in other words, they do not have the right kind of faith. Most of us think that faith is belief: *I believe and so therefore I have faith.* Jesus says that if you had what he calls faith, you would only need as much as a mustard seed. What is a mustard seed? It is the tiniest seed you can possibly imagine. With just that much, you could do astonishing things and he gives this example of the mulberry tree being planted into the sea. What does that mean?

The French translation from the Greek is: *"Tell that mulberry tree, pull yourself up by your roots as a tree and go plant yourself in the ocean."* In other words, you can do impossible things with the right kind of faith. But what kind of faith is it? The word for "faith" in Greek means *to make obey*, to make ourselves obey. Earlier, Jesus says to disciples when they cannot heal someone: **"Faithless and perverse generation."** The Greek for *perverse* means -- *you who turn in every direction.* One moment we feel like this, another minute we feel like that.

We are fragmented. We are not united. All of our powers which could be used for good are "turning in every direction." We cannot count on ourselves. We are inconsistent. Jesus is telling us that real faith is to make all these different parts of ourselves obey the desire to love God and to follow these teachings. We are called to develop joyful obedience, delight in applying the teachings of God. The Spirit can then work with you. Can you imagine the Spirit trying to work with someone who is completely undependable? Out of that little mustard seed of desire and commitment grows the greatest tree in the field. Out of the smallest act that you do in the name of God can come great miracles.

15

LET YOUR LIGHT SHINE:
THE PARABLE OF SALT AND LIGHT
Matthew 5: 13-17

'You are the salt of the earth; but if salt has lost its taste, how can its saltiness be restored? It is no longer good for anything, but is thrown out and trampled under foot. 'You are the light of the world. A city built on a hill cannot be hidden. No one after lighting a lamp puts it under the bushel basket, but on the lamp stand, and it gives light to all in the house. In the same way, let your light shine before others, so that they may see your good works and give glory to your Father in heaven. 'Do not think that I have come to abolish the law or the prophets; I have come not to abolish but to fulfill.

We have here another teaching from the Savior. Why do we call him Savior? Because he reveals to all of us, to all humanity, the reality of God, the reality of ourselves, and enables us to be new people while we live in a world of pain and struggle. He enables us to rise up to a more noble life, to the life that was planned for us before we were born.

Several verses back, Jesus offers us two metaphors. One is salt, the other is light. You have heard the saying, "**You are the salt of the earth,**" and we sometimes throw that around, not quite sure what it means.

Salt in the first century was extremely valuable. In fact, Roman soldiers were often paid their wages in salt. Salt was the only preservative for food. Salt in those days kept meat from smelling bad and what Jesus is saying to us is that we need salt in our lives to keep us from smelling bad. Human beings left to themselves without this spiritual salt will decay, and each of us must admit to ourselves that in some areas of our life, we do not smell so good. Jesus says: "*If you love God, if you have begun to discover who you are spiritually, you have become salty. You have begun to preserve yourself from decay.*"

Consider people who are so unhappy, so bitter, that they want to spread it around to everyone else. There is no salt in such behavior. Jesus says, "**What is salt good for if it has lost its saltiness?**" It gets thrown out. It gets trampled under foot. This is a warning to us.

To be light, to be salt is to be over against the world. Jesus is not telling us to remove ourselves but he certainly is telling us not to be like the world. If everyone around believes it is all right to be intolerant, to hate, to belittle, to be always complaining, they are enacting the words of Jesus: *What is salt worth if it has lot its saltiness?*

116

The Greek word for "loses its saltiness" is *moraino* which gives us the English word "moron". Jesus is saying that we live foolishly if we do not have the salt of spiritual character. You have got to work at it. You have got to find out where things are decaying in your soul, in your heart. If you cannot forgive, there is decay. If you want to have salt, to be salt in the world, you know what you must do. You have got to step up, overcome the downward pull of your character. Remember, if there is no salt, things rot. The world without spirit rots.

What is more horrible than the selfishness that keeps the world a hellish place? When Jesus says **"you are the salt of the earth, you are the light of the world,"** he is saying: *If you love God, if you have begun to step out of the way everyone else lives, and to make spirit important to your life, then you have a job to do.*

Salt does not do any good if it stays in the saltshaker. It has to be poured out. If you are seeking God, if you are trying to live according to the ways revealed by Jesus to the world, then you need to let your light shine. You need to make life around you tasty like salt. You need to make people thirsty for God because of the person you are. Imagine if you were able to make people around you wonder, *"What is it that they've got? How can they keep their peace when things are awful? I get all crazy but they stay peaceful. They know something. I want what they know. I want what they have."* Make people thirsty for God!

Do you realize that what Jesus is saying to us is that God -- this mystery beyond comprehension -- needs us to shed light, to make a difference in this world, to not be of the world but to care for the world. We first care for the world by being different: Why is this person more humble? Why is this person happy all the time? You can have joy and the knowledge that God is in every moment and that, no matter what happens to you, all your worries can be put aside. That is power. That is salt. That is light.

When Jesus says "**you are the light of the world**," he is not saying that each of us is a divine light, a special light. We all know what we are. The Bible calls us earthen vessels. We are lamps and in those oil lamps, you need to put oil. What is the oil? The ancient teachers tell us it is the Holy Spirit. It is the creative act of God in our life that can fill each one of us.

You need to have a little zeal, a little passion to get off the couch of comfortable living, of selfish living and become a light for God in this world. The word "enthusiasm" in Greek is *en theos*, meaning "in God." Enthusiasm is to be in God and it only takes a few people who get excited about the idea of goodness above selfishness, of forgiveness above bitterness, to salt the world.

What is the world without a few people who are trying to make a difference? Do we want to leave it to the darkness that it is? Without spirit, without self-transcendence, without getting over ourselves so that we stand for something greater than ourselves, this world is sunk. In every culture, in every land, there is hunger for meaning, hunger for something beautiful about life.

Science is not the answer. Progress is not the answer. One new computer gadget is not going to make this a better palace. *You* are the answer. You -- in the simplest way, in the smallest way, being a bit of light in a world of such unhappiness. It means to be contagious, with joy, with peace, with love. It just takes a few of us. God is calling you to be that salt. Everyday of your life can be one more step towards bringing light into this world.

Jesus tells us: Do not take a lit lamp and put it under a cover. We have to risk proving that we do not need a safety net to go out there and to believe that all will be well, that we are protected, that we are loved, that there are angels of goodness around us. Who will dare to believe that? Life is full of wonder, full of potential, full of mystery and the center of it is in your soul.

Carl Sagan, the astronomer who did not believe in God, did say that each one of us was the center of the expansion of the universe. This expansion is happening in the center of our being. We are star stuff. We are awesome creatures placed here to be God's light while we live and breathe in this brief passage through time. When Jesus says: *What happens to salt that loses its saltiness?* He is asking us: How can we be spiritual people without a hunger and a zeal for the things of God? Let's do away with religion that is flat.

The world needs us now to be alive, alive in spirit to dare to risk for God. We do not fulfill God's plan for us and for the world until we stand up and are counted as that remnant of humanity that says "yes" to God. We are all called to this, not to retreat from the world but to stand in the midst of it and offer an alternative perspective. To be salt, to be light is just to be good when nobody else cares about being good, to be the one who does not get angry when everyone is upset.

This is why Jesus came. To call together a few people who would dare to try this, who would dare to overcome their own limitations and let God's light come through them. We only reflect the light of God. You do not need anything special but the desire for it, the hunger for it. Then you can transform your world beginning with your heart and your family, your neighborhood, your world. Let your light shine. That is what you are here for. Let your light shine and you will know the blessing of God in your life and become blessing to others.

16

THE COST:
THE PARABLE OF THE BUILDER AND THE KING
Luke 14: 25-33

Now large crowds were travelling with him; and he turned and said to them, 'Whoever comes to me and does not hate father and mother, wife and children, brothers and sisters, yes, and even life itself, cannot be my disciple. Whoever does not carry the cross and follow me cannot be my disciple. For which of you, intending to build a tower, does not first sit down and estimate the cost, to see whether he has enough to complete it? Otherwise, when he has laid a foundation and is not able to finish, all who see it will begin to ridicule him, saying, "This fellow began to build and was not able to finish." Or what king, going out to wage war against another king, will not sit down first and consider whether he is able with ten thousand to oppose the one who comes against him with twenty thousand? If he cannot, then, while the other is still far away, he sends a delegation and asks for the terms of peace. So therefore, none of you can become my disciple if you do not give up all your possessions.

121

What kind of a teaching is this? What about that love and comfort and grace business? We are confronted with these hard and disturbing words, giving us specific instructions. Like the crowd, we may also want to find someone else to follow.

Notice that he is surrounded by a large crowd. He has done some amazing things. There is good reason to follow him, but now he says something which is so shocking that it guarantees many are going to leave. This is further complicated by the fact that we find in the Old Testament the following words from the prophet Malachi, the one who prophesied that the Messiah would come: **"He will restore the hearts of the parents to their children and the hearts of the children to their parents."**

How does that connect with what we find here in this teaching?
When Jesus speaks of "hating father and mother," we must remember that he is speaking in Aramaic. The word *hate* is just a translation into English of Aramaic, a Semitic language full of hyperbole.

If you look at Genesis chapter 29, there is a story of Jacob who loved Rachel more than Leah and you find this very same word: *"He hated Leah."* Right after that verse, we find out that he had seven more children with Leah. What kind of hate is that?

In the Gospel of Matthew, this same teaching is given with a positive spin: **"You must love me more than**

mother and father, children, wife…" So Jesus is saying something of great significance that is hard to grasp. You must detach yourself from the love of these people who are so close to you. Pull back so that your first priority, your first love, your first commitment is to God. We have the saying in this world that "blood is thicker than water" and we put a lot of pride in that family closeness, as did the Hatfield and the McCoys. They had lots of family love, but just for their own. They hated everyone else. How many of us have defined our identity as a human being over against our family? How many of us have spent a lifetime trying to please a mother or a father?

Sometimes you have to pull away so that you can come back and love them from a different place. So what Jesus is saying is that we need to love Love itself. We need to love the source of love, to love Unconditional Love, and then we can love mother and father, brother, sister, children from that place. In other words, it enables us to love all these people even better. This is completely different from the literal reading of this key teaching. At the end of this passage, Jesus says, "**Let those who have ears hear what I am saying.**" Let it be clear Jesus is not telling us to have emotional revulsion toward another person. He is saying that, in order to enter the way of life that he came to reveal to every human being, the first priority must be the living God through Whom we are enabled to truly love, to truly forgive, to truly walk the way of Christ.

We find then that he tells us, "**Whoever does not carry the cross and follow me cannot be my disciple.**" In the secular world, we have heard this term "bearing our

123

cross" and used it in a way that does not really fit what Jesus meant. We use the term for chronic illness, or as enduring (bearing) the cross of someone else in a bad relationship. That is not what Jesus is teaching us. To bear your cross as a spiritual person means to *deliberately choose to sacrifice for the sake of God's ways*. It means to intentionally make an effort you would not otherwise make.

The Gospel of Luke tells us that a spiritual person, a lover of God, a follower of Christ should bear their cross *daily*. We must each day start again in surrendering to God. Then we begin to realize what this cost is about, the cost that Jesus refers to through metaphor, trying to identify for us the personal sacrifice that we must make internally in order to truly be able to know God.

We all have scars. We have all made mistakes. We have all experienced unfairness done to us in such a way that we want to curl up and hide, or to strike out, or to control things. In all those ways, what we really do is cut God out of our life because we are not willing and free enough to become dependent on that goodness alone.

Jesus is saying you have to pay the cost of letting go of that place in your heart where God cannot get in. This is not just for specific disciples of Jesus. This is God's gift to every human being so that we can live in a joy and peace that nothing can destroy.

He goes on to tell us, **"Which of you who are intending to build a tower does not first sit and estimate the cost?"** In other words, he is telling us there is something that we have to do, a process that we must go through. So we have to do something and the doing of that something is not external. It is internal.

Then he goes on to tell us that we are like the king who is going to face an army. Why does he use that example about a king facing another king with a larger army who is sure to be massacred? This is a matter of life and death.

Do you know that one of the great sacrifices of life is to have joy even when nothing is going your way? To have joy because *God is*. That is the cost. That is the calculation of what we need to do in order enter the way of Christ.

Finally, he tells us, "**So therefore, none of you can become my disciple if you do not give up all your possessions.**" This is the very same thing we have seen with the words, "**If you do not hate your mother and father.**" It does not mean what it seems to say. It does not mean putting on a giant yard sale and becoming a beggar in the streets. What good are you going to be to others if you have nothing left? That is silliness, yet for centuries, we have had this ingrained thinking that this is what he must mean. Rather, Jesus is telling us: *"Don't be possessed by your possessions. Don't make happiness your stuff because you just might lose it."*

If God is the source of your happiness, your real possession, then everything else falls into place. God does not love the poor more than the rich. God loves everyone – this is the meaning of unconditional love. Jesus is teaching spiritual detachment. He is giving you the keys, the secret, the power to survive in this world by tapping in to the main power source, the one that does not go out when the trees fall on the lines.

But we constantly keep ourselves disconnected by grabbing on to other things for security. Dare to let go and fly. That is what Jesus is telling you. Dare to let go and trust without a safety net that God is good. Then you are in the company of Jesus, then your fears and your worries are wiped out because you are trusting in the goodness of God.

17

WATCHFULNESS:
THE PARABLE OF THE VIGILANT SERVANTS
Luke 12: 35-39

'Be dressed for action and have your lamps lit; be like those who are waiting for their master to return from the wedding banquet, so that they may open the door for him as soon as he comes and knocks. Blessed are those slaves whom the master finds alert when he comes; truly I tell you, he will fasten his belt and have them sit down to eat, and he will come and serve them. If he comes during the middle of the night, or near dawn, and finds them so, blessed are those slaves.

'But know this: if the owner of the house had known at what hour the thief was coming, he would not have let his house be broken into.

We have here before us one of the most specific and powerful instructions given to us by the Savior. This is a teaching moment out of eternity for each one of us but it is in spiritual language and therefore we must decode it like any other parable. The translation says *be dressed for action and have your lamps lit.*

This is where we go beyond the surface, thinking from the sense-based mind, into thinking with the spiritual mind. When Jesus teaches: "**Be dressed for action and have your lamps lit**," he is referring to a battle of the mind. It is an internal battle with yourself. The lamp to be lit is your awareness. Being dressed for action is being prepared and alert. In this great teaching that we find in Matthew, Mark and Luke, we hear the words *watch, be alert, be awake.*

Our reality is that we live on automatic. We live in our habits. We live in response to external stimuli. Jesus is telling us in no uncertain terms to wake up, to light those lamps of attention so that we can become unified and conscious of God.

There is no escape from what this teaching means. It is a hard one because it is difficult to apply. We are constantly responding to stimulus without any willpower. We hear Proverbs saying: "**Blessed is the one who waits at my door.**" These are beautiful poetic words dealing with spiritual matters which relate directly, immediately to our lives.

To keep your lamp lit is to remember God, to remember how you are meant to live. You cannot remember God and be nasty at the same time. You cannot rage at your kid, kick the dog, hate the neighbor and love God at the same time.

If you control yourself in the holy name of Jesus, you become a different person. You become the person you are meant to be. You become a person capable of contact with spiritual reality. All of us live outside of ourselves, always seeing and responding, never present within, self-aware, self-controlled, remembering God. This is the teaching.

We are then told: "**Be like those waiting for their master to return, ready to open the door immediately as soon as he shows up.**" What does this marvelous metaphor mean? Can you imagine a moment in your life when the Holy Spirit is seeking to get into your consciousness, to get into your heart but you are not home? Let's say you've prayed for help. Let's say you have said: "*God, I want to know you. Help me.*"

Spirit shows up at your back door but you are too busy. You are too caught up with an emotion. You are too lost in the world. You are thinking about your laundry. You are in traffic. God shows up in your life and He cannot get through to you because your lamp is not lit, because you are not waiting for Him. This is no theory. Do not wait until the last moment, a moment of great grief, of great terror, to finally shut down everything else and say: "*God, here I am. Come to me.*"

Jesus says, "**Blessed is the one whom the master finds alert when he arrives.**" Think about that. A universal,

129

eternal teaching saying to us: *You are fortunate, you are blessed.* Happy are you, to be envied, are you -- that is what *blessed* means -- if you are alert, awake, not lost into all your emotions of anger and bitterness, boredom, resentment, criticizing, judgment. Blessed are you if you are alert, seeking God, making room for God when He shows up in your life.

We are then told that the Master will have you sit down to eat with him. What do you think that means? Communion, eating with God, relating with the Spirit. But he goes even further. He says, **"And that Master will serve you."** The spirit, the force of the universe, will not only come to you, He will not only interact with you. He will serve you. He will care for you. This is the teaching of Jesus to us. This is the revelation that no other teaching gives us.

If you want the greatest wisdom of the world, here it is encoded in these simple images that we have heard a million times and never understood because it is all about what we are doing in the ordinary moments of our lives. Jesus takes it a step further. He switches metaphors on us.

He says, **"Know this. If the owner of the house knew what time the thief was going to break in, he would be ready for him."** This is where it switches. The owner of the house is you, your true self, the person you have always been and can remember back to your earliest days. There is a self in us that transcends all the stages of our lives.

You are the owner of your house and Jesus says, "**Know this, that if you knew when the thief was going to come**." Imagine a moment of urgency, and you were ready for the intrusion of the enemy. Who is the enemy? What is the intrusion?

There is an early saying, an early version of this teaching from the Gospel of Thomas that states, "**Fortunate is the one who knows where the thief will enter**." Let me translate that for you: *Fortunate are you who knows where your weak spots are, where your anger will rise or your hatred will emerge.* Happy is the one who knows himself or herself well enough to know where the thief of your soul is going to come in.

That is the battle of the mind: Choosing which thought you are going to go with, which emotion you are going to let ravage you, take center stage, which self is going to be in control, which one is going to be awake when the thief comes.

We are being robbed all the time and our life force is stolen from us. Have you ever felt what it is like to be really angry? How it wears you out? Jesus is trying to show you another way, another path, another life. Peter says, "*What do you mean by this?*" because he is in the same boat as we are. What are you talking about with these images? And Jesus says again, "**Truly I say to you, blessed is the one whom the master finds alert when he arrives**." He then teaches: "**He will put him in charge of all his possessions**." What do you think that means? To be put in charge of all of God's things, to be able to handle life, to be able to survive suffering, crisis, the unexpected, to be in charge of yourself so that you can deal with life. That is the result of being awake, of the inner warfare with your self, knowing what part of you is stealing your soul, knowing what part of you needs to have that lamp lit.

But then Jesus goes on. He talks about the servant who says, **"Well, my master is delayed."** He thinks that there is no hurry, but in spiritual matters, there is no tomorrow. There is only now. God lives in the Now. This is the time to awaken from sleep, to arise from the dead, from a life where there is no God. There is no time to lose. You have a choice in every moment of your life.

Jesus tells that the servant who says the master is delayed goes on and gets drunk, beats the other servants (which means he lives any way he wants), will suffer consequences. The Prince of Peace says: **"He will receive a severe beating."** This is a metaphor. God is not going to punch you out. But it is punishment nevertheless, and in Proverbs we read: **"Those who do not seek me, those who don't find me, those who miss me, injure themselves."** You injure yourself by not finding God.

Then Jesus tells us: **"To all who have been given, much will be demanded."** The servant who did not know what his master wanted will get just a little beating. The servant who knows what the master wanted and was not prepared or did not do what was required, will be cast out with the hypocrites, the unfaithful, the unbeliev-

132

ers. The literal translation reads: **"He will be cut to pieces."**

You have been given the teaching from Jesus to wake up, to not let yourself get away with just any behavior, not merely because it is unpleasant, but because it cuts God out of your life. So Jesus says, **"Therefore I say to you, keep awake."**

PARABLE WISDOM

18

THE DEEP:
THE PARABLE OF THE NET
Luke 5: 1-11

Once while Jesus was standing beside the lake of Gennesaret, and the crowd was pressing in on him to hear the word of God, he saw two boats there at the shore of the lake; the fishermen had gone out of them and were washing their nets. He got into one of the boats, the one belonging to Simon, and asked him to put out a little way from the shore. Then he sat down and taught the crowds from the boat. When he had finished speaking, he said to Simon, 'Put out into the deep water and let down your nets for a catch.' Simon answered, 'Master, we have worked all night long but have caught nothing. Yet if you say so, I will let down the nets.' When they had done this, they caught so many fish that their nets were beginning to break. So they signaled to their partners in the other boat to come and help them. And they came and filled both boats, so that they began to sink. But when Simon Peter saw it, he fell down at Jesus' knees, saying, 'Go away from me, Lord, for I am a sinful man!' For he and all who were with him were amazed at the catch of fish that they had taken; and so also were James and John, sons of

Zebedee, who were partners with Simon. Then Jesus said to Simon, 'Do not be afraid; from now on you will be catching people.' When they had brought their boats to shore, they left everything and followed him.

This is a story about becoming disciples, becoming Christians, people of the Way as they were called before the word "Christian" was used. This was a teaching on how to do it, therefore it is not about the twelve disciples. It is about you and me as we seek to be true to the Truth that we believe in, that we feel in our hearts as the essence of why we are here.

Jesus comes and teaches people from the boat. But did you notice that it does not mention what he said? There is no teaching expressed here. That tells us that the story itself is the teaching. As 21st century people, you know that when you take a four gigabyte file and turn it to a 100 megabyte file, you have compressed a great amount of information. That is what we have here. This is sacred wisdom containing universal truth and one of our great mistakes is that we only take it on the surface.

For hundreds of years, for centuries, all the teachers talked about different levels of understanding holy scripture and yet, somewhere around the 1800s, scholars locked in to merely the surface, leaving us with a story about Peter and the guys out fishing. Yet, this is only a picture to touch us at an emotional level that can understand better than our mind. Jesus is bypassing our mind to a place where we can understand in another way.

Let me give you an example of a picture that stirs the emotions. You notice that the fishermen were washing their nets and a bit later, we find Peter saying, "**We've worked hard all night and haven't caught anything**." Have you ever tried something with all your efforts and gotten nowhere? Have you ever run out of steam or lost hope? Have you ever given up on something because you've given it all you had and nothing came of it?

Jesus is addressing us right there in that frustrated place, in that unhappy place, in that depressed place, whatever it is that caused it. Jesus is giving us a spiritual remedy to our sense of failure.

We too spent the night fishing and did not catch anything, each in our own way. He gives us the key to how we can get past that failure, that hopelessness. You will notice that Peter addresses him as "Master" but has never met him before. Here is the simple fisherman looking up at this man covered with dust from Galilee and, somehow, he knows that he is looking at a holy man. Can you imagine for a moment what must have been radiating out of this man to cause the fisherman with no education to call him "Master"?

Yet even though he called him Master, he knew his business when it came to fishing. He knew that fishing should take place at night when the fish were up by the surface, rather than in the day, when they scatter down into the depths. Yet this holy man, who is not a fisherman, is telling him his business. All of us think we know something about the things that interest us. We have our little corner carved out that we know all about, and here comes Jesus messing with our business, telling us something that is not logical. Nevertheless, Peter says, "**Yet because you say so, we will do it.**" That is a sacred teaching: *I don't understand it, I don't know where it's going to lead m,. it's not familiar, it's not what I know but because you say so, I will do it.*

Consider a situation in your life where, in applying this teaching, another door will open, another opportunity will arise "because you say so." Look at the fruits of the Spirit: *Because you say to be patient even though I'm so upset and it makes no sense and I'm right and they're wrong, yet I will be patient.*

Try it some time. This is the effort that opens the door to the other side, to a new life, to God's way in our life. If you want to get out of a dead end -- spiritual, emotional, intellectual -- this is how you do it: Do what God tells you to do even if it makes no sense. Can you manifest enough faith, enough trust in the God revealed by Jesus to say, "*If you say so, I will do it, I will have faith?*"

Peter responds: "Okay, makes no sense but if you say so, I'll do it." And what happens? They go out in the middle of the day time and the net gets so full, it starts breaking. There are so many fish that the other boat comes out to help and the two boats start sinking. Now what does this picture tell us? This is what the mercy of God is like! This is the abundance of Grace with which God wants to fill our life. This is what God wants to give each of us.

If Peter had not said "if you say so," if he had said, *"I'm sorry, rabbi. We tried it. We can't do it,"* Jesus would be on his way to find himself another fisherman, another community, another set of people who might just be willing to go out and take the risk. But Peter did say it and the simple fisherman is known to us today as one of the great world transformers. God will take anyone of us and use us for His purposes if we are willing like Peter to say, *"Okay, I'll do it."* That decision opens the door, and makes the impossible possible.

We love those words – **"For God all things are possible."** But the application is another matter: *I'm in a terrible relationship. We're going to get divorced. It's never going to work.* That is when those words need to become real for us. That is when you must think of abundance that fills the ships and the nets to overflowing. That is the word of Jesus. This is not a fantasy, nor poetry. It is the power of God.

Peter sees this astonishing miracle, this manifestation of the Holy and he falls on his knees, not to worship but to beg Jesus to go away. He wants Jesus to get away from him! What does that mean? When you and I are faced with Truth, with purity, with goodness, it is like placing a mirror right up to everything that is not so pure within us. We do not want to see ourselves. Our response most often is: *"Get away from me, please. I would much rather be comfortable in my old ways, in my darkness."* Jesus is too much to handle especially if you do not want to follow his life-changing teachings.

139

So here is this man who is so ashamed of himself, of just being a human being that he says — "*You shouldn't be around me.*" And what does Jesus say to you, to me? "**Do not be afraid.**" God loves us anyway. The Holy accepts us despite ourselves and will use anyway in all our fragmentation, brokenness, confusion and mistakes. If we are willing, God wants us to sign up and be part of God's activity in the world no matter who we are. That is why we were born.

Then comes the next lesson: "**From now on, you will catch people.**" The Greek words translate more literally as: "From now on, you will revive people, bring them back to life."

He is telling us: *From now on, you will go out into the deep, the dangerous, where people don't believe anything, are lost, are in turmoil, are surrounded by sharks. Go out into the deep and go get them.* That is the mission of the disciple: I will send you into all the depths, starting with next door. There are many fish out there who are hungry for God, who are lost without God. Perhaps more than ever before, we are a disintegrating society, a broken civilization and the words of Jesus tell us: *Help them find God, help them find peace, help them find joy and sanity.* The assumption is that we find sanity first so that there is a sane place for them to come.

That is the message of Jesus in black and white: Bring people into contact with God and you will be feeding thousands. And what happens? The disciples leave everything and follow him. This means that the disciples freed themselves of everything. To follow him, you have to deny yourself, release your self from your own need to be right all the time, to be in charge, to have your own way - - all those desires that make you inaccessible to the Holy Spirit.

This is how you are transformed. This is how you become a light in this world so that others will want what you have found.

PARABLE WISDOM

19

THE MIRACLE AS PARABLE:
WATER INTO WINE
John 2: 1-11

On the third day there was a wedding in Cana of Galilee, and the mother of Jesus was there. Jesus and his disciples had also been invited to the wedding. When the wine gave out, the mother of Jesus said to him, 'They have no wine.' And Jesus said to her, 'Woman, what concern is that to you and to me? My hour has not yet come.' His mother said to the servants, 'Do whatever he tells you.' Now standing there were six stone water-jars for the Jewish rites of purification, each holding twenty or thirty gallons. Jesus said to them, 'Fill the jars with water.' And they filled them up to the brim. He said to them, 'Now draw some out, and take it to the chief steward.' So they took it. When the steward tasted the water that had become wine, and did not know where it came from (though the servants who had drawn the water knew), the steward called the bridegroom and said to him, 'Everyone serves the good wine first, and then the inferior wine after the guests have become drunk. But you have kept the good wine until now.' Jesus did this, the first of his signs, in Cana of Gali-

lee, and revealed his glory; and his disciples believed in him.

These are indeed words of the Lord, sacred scripture, holy scripture, words that have to be read in the tradition of *lectio divina,* with prayerful intent and attention because they carry such depth, such wonderful meaning beyond the surface. This is a classic example of how rich scripture truly is if we enter it, if we let it speak to our heart and to our spirit. So let us put aside the assumption that this is just a miracle. All throughout the Gospel of John, miracles are signs pointing to something beyond themselves. This teaching points to something else as well, something that has direct impact on each of us.

I will begin by pointing out a few clues to the depths of this teaching. First, when you hear of a wedding, typically you find out the identity of the bride and groom. They play an important role in that event. Can you imagine going to a wedding not knowing who the bride and groom are? Yet, there is not a word concerning them in this story of a wedding. It is not about them. It is not about the wedding. It concerns a union, a spiritual union. Second, this is the little tiny village of Cana, six miles north of Galilee. We do not hear of it any place else. In this tiny village with its little wedding, we have a story that includes six hundred bottles of wine.

This teaching is rich with Hebrew symbolism and spiritual wisdom. It begins with the words – "**On the third day.**" In Hebrew numerology or gematria, the number three is very significant. It implies the beginning, middle, end. Three is completion, fulfillment, new beginning.

We find the number three in other places: "**On the third day, he rose again.**" How many days was Jonah in the whale? Would you believe three days? How many times did Peter deny his master? Three times. To every Hebrew of that era, it meant *fully and completely.* So "on the third day" means *in this moment of new beginnings* -- a fulfillment of prophecy and purpose.

At the wedding, the mother of Jesus points out that they have no more wine. Wine is used throughout the Old Testament as a symbol of joy. In ancient times, it was a blessing from the earth, one that enabled relaxation and rejoicing. It was part of the fullness of life. So wine was joy, and abundance of wine was great joy. It was such great joy that it stood for the Messianic days, which is why the prophet Amos says: "**On that day** (which is the appearance of the Anointed One in the world)**, new wine shall drip from the mountains and fall from the hills.**" The wine represents the delight of our soul.

Mary says: "**Standing in front of thee, six stone water jars for the rites of purification.**" These jars represent the religion of the Hebrews, the ancient religion. When she says that they have no more wine, the symbolic meaning is that the religion has become barren. It has been four hundred years since a prophet from God walked the land.

Surely, you are a bit surprised when you hear Jesus say, "**Woman…**" Let me point out that he says "woman" at another time -- on the cross -- saying, "**Woman, behold your son**," speaking of the Apostle John standing there in despair. So the term "woman" is not a negative, although it is an objectification because this new beginning represents Jesus of Nazareth, son of Joseph and Mary, becoming Jesus the Christ, son of the living God. He is moving from his natural identity into his true identity.

This is a message telling you that you are not merely the product of your Mom and Dad. You are not the result of whatever mistakes they made. You are not just the imitation of their ways. You are not merely what your environment created. You are more than your DNA. You are child of the living God. As the Gospel of John says: "**What is born of flesh is flesh; what is born a spirit, is spirit.**" When you awaken to your true identity, to your spiritual self, you find that you are much more than just that person you thought you were.

Jesus says, according to this translation, something like, "**What does this have to do with you and me?**" You will find all sorts of politically correct, cleaned-up, watered-down versions of that statement.

The King James version took it straight from the Greek and it says, "**Woman, what have I to do with thee?**" The French Bible, taking it from the Greek, states: "**What is there between you and me?**" So Jesus is distancing himself fully from his mother – from her call to action. He says, "**My hour has not yet come.**" He re-

146

moves himself from the human pull on his life so that he can be fully anchored in the Spirit, in the inspiration of Spirit, in the guidance of Spirit.

He is standing before six water jars. The number six is full of meaning -- six days of preparation to the Sabbath, six days of creation, six years of servitude before the servant was freed, six steps to the temple of Solomon. The number expresses a time of preparation for the coming of the Lord, for the fullness of time.

Here we have a reference to this ancient religion going back to Abraham, to the dawn of humanity -- waiting in preparation for the Messiah, for this new dispensation, this new revelation of God. Notice that these are stone jars, like the stone tablets of the Ten Commandments.

In spiritual symbolism, there are three levels of truth: stone, water, wine. Stone truth is found in: *Thou shall not kill and if thou killest, we will kill thee.* It is literal truth, often a truth with no mercy, a truth that we must obey, and much religion is simply truth of stone -- follow the laws or else. Water, which also stands for Truth, is found when we begin to recognize the good of the Teaching, the good of God's Word, the good of not killing -- not because we are afraid of what will happen but because it is the right thing to do. It is the beginning of transformation. Christ tells us, *"You have heard it said...but I say to you; you have heard it said 'Do not kill,' I say to you, do not even think deadly thoughts about your neighbor in your mind."*

Understand that since it is wine, it is the kind of truth that intoxicates the soul. It gives you joy to live out the teachings of Christ. That is wine. This is what Jesus brings into the world, not a religion of laws, not a morality of obligation, but a delighting in spirit. This kind of Truth naturally makes us good people, forgiving people, caring people.

Now we come to the meaning of the marriage, the union. It is a marriage between what we know and what is in our character. When knowledge and being come together, a new understanding is created.

So the secret formula to spiritual transformation is the application of what you know through living it out. This is the union which creates the person we are called to be. Jesus changes us into wine. When you bring the teachings into your life, you can bring flavor and joy that were not there before.

This is the miracle. Not out there in Cana at a wedding but right in the middle of your life. Living out the power that the Christ has brought into the world, the renewal of what religion is meant to be. The secret is in the very first step, the very beginning of Christ's ministry in the Gospel of John. On that "third day" comes a new beginning, not just for Jesus, for all of us.

20

THE MIRACLE AS PARABLE:
LOAVES AND FISHES
John 6: 1-14

After this Jesus went to the other side of the Sea of Galilee, also called the Sea of Tiberias. A large crowd kept following him, because they saw the signs that he was doing for the sick. Jesus went up the mountain and sat down there with his disciples. Now the Passover, the festival of the Jews, was near. When he looked up and saw a large crowd coming towards him, Jesus said to Philip, 'Where are we to buy bread for these people to eat?' He said this to test him, for he himself knew what he was going to do. Philip answered him, 'Six months' wages would not buy enough bread for each of them to get a little.' One of his disciples, Andrew, Simon Peter's brother, said to him, 'There is a boy here who has five barley loaves and two fish. But what are they among so many people?' Jesus said, 'Make the people sit down.' Now there was a great deal of grass in the place; so they sat down, about five thousand in all. Then Jesus took the loaves, and when he had given thanks, he distributed them to those who were seated; so also the fish, as much as they wanted. When they were satisfied, he told his disciples,

'Gather up the fragments left over, so that nothing may be lost.' So they gathered them up, and from the fragments of the five barley loaves, left by those who had eaten, they filled twelve baskets. When the people saw the sign that he had done, they began to say, 'This is indeed the prophet who is to come into the world.'

We all know this story. It is a beautiful picture of Jesus at the height of that bringing forth of the glory of God. We love those miracles and they touch our hearts but they are so much more than that. We could spend a lifetime studying this teaching and discover new depths of wisdom for our lives. This is not just a story about Jesus, a first century happening. This is a divine wisdom teaching, a revelation from the one we called the Savior so that it can be applied today to your life. Otherwise, it is not Holy Scripture. Holy Scripture is power. "**My words are spirit and they are life**," Jesus says later on in this chapter.

We hear about the great crowds that followed him. Do you know that at the end of this chapter, they all abandoned him including most of his disciples? Look at John 6:66, strangely enough, where we are told that most of the disciples would have nothing more to do with him. So there is a great deal more going on here than a wonderful miracle sign of God's presence. This is a powerful teaching. Let me show you how multi-layered it is, how symbolic this imagery. We read that Jesus goes up a mountain. Be sure that, in the first century, no one went to the top of the mountain to have a picnic. Mountains were frightening places, haunted places, places that civilization did not go near, places where only a few lonely prophets wandered. The mountain has been a symbol throughout the Old Testament of the high place where one goes to be close to God. It reminds us of the might and wonder of the Holy One.

So whenever we hear that Jesus goes up a mountain, it is for the purpose of giving us a revelation. We find the Master asking Philip: *"How are we going to feed all these people?"* For one of the few times in Holy Scripture, we are given a clue. We are told: **"He said this as a test."** But we need to understand that it was not a test for Philip. It is a test for us.

Five thousand people, no food -- What does this mean? Answer: Big problem. What are you dealing with now that is a problem? That is the test. Philip was the one who said in the previous chapter: **"You are the one that Moses spoke of."** He recognizes the Messiah so long awaited and yet here in this moment, he does not understand. And what does he not understand? The same thing we do not understand in our problems. When we are facing a crisis, we try to figure it out on our own. It is up to us to fix it, to make it work. We are like the two-year-old: *I'll do it myself.* What is missing in all this? The Presence, guidance and purpose of God in the midst of our problem.

We may believe in God but when it is time to place God at the center of our reality, somehow we generally fail to do that. Like Philip, we miss the opportunity. Philip thinks he needs to run to a bakery down the road in Bethsaida and order five thousand loaves of bread.

He failed the test. He failed to realize that in Jesus, in the incarnation of God among us, we find the answer. He failed to say: "*Lord, you can do it, You can do whatever is needed to be done.*" Have you ever gotten to that point in your life, in your problem to say, "*Lord, I leave it to you*"? Isn't that a beautiful moment in your life? Isn't that a release, a peace, a faith that empowers you, that takes away the fear and the torment and the anxiety which makes life such misery?

The next teaching comes to us in the form of a little boy. We all know the story -- five barley loaves and two fishes. Why five? Why not four? I remind you of the five books of the Torah, the books of Moses. We are shown here how the Christ brings that manna from heaven in a way that Moses could never do. This little boy offers these barley loaves. And what is a barley loaf? It is bread unfit for human consumption. It is for the animals. It is bad bread so we have some bad bread and some tiny sardines and five thousand people. What does this represent? Impossible odds, an insignificant thing that is supposed to solve an impossible situation. Here is the teaching: It is in the insignificant thing, in your gift, in your stepping up to the plate and saying, "*God, I'll help,*" that the miracle happens.

No matter what you have to offer, no matter how little you know, no matter how many mistakes you have made in the past, God only wants to see a willing heart and out of a wiling heart, God will make a miracle in this world. So do not think that you are not the one because you are that one just like that boy who had so little to offer and yet so much to give God.

Now we come to the point of the miracle. What initiates this awesome moment? Jesus gives thanks. He gives thanks in this hopeless situation. He says, "Thank you Lord," and that is a teaching. When you are in a situation that you do not like, where God does not seem to be giving you what you need, if you say thank you anyway, the miracle will happen for you. The great mystic, Meister Eckhart, tells us that if the only prayer we can say is thank you, that will be enough. The gratitude that nothing can shake will yield a miracle in your life.

The miracle takes place. And what are we told? The people are not merely fed. They are fed until they are so full that they do not want anymore, and once they have been completely filled, there is a great deal left over. What does this picture mean? God blesses beyond our wildest imagination. God's grace is overabundant.

We ask for a little something from God and amazing things happen because the God revealed by Jesus brings blessings beyond our wildest dreams. So they gather the leftovers. And what do we have? Twelve baskets. Why not nine baskets? Seven baskets? The number twelve -- twelve patriarchs, twelve disciples -- is a holy number which represents the perfection of God in the world. Jesus tells them to gather it all together so that none will be wasted. What does that mean? That every act of God's grace is never wasted. Every moment of random kindness in the universe makes a difference. God's grace will reach everyone who is receptive to it. Nothing is wasted in this universe. We know that in our ecologically-minded world today. We are worried about our carbon footprint. We know everything affects everything else. We know about recycling. Jesus tells us, in the first century, nothing of God's holiness and grace is wasted. It is all used for good.

This crowd, which has been filled with good food, hurries after Jesus and he turns to them and says, *"You want more bread. We filled your stomach with bread. That's why you're following me. I am the bread, I am the living bread."* That is when everyone stops and says, *"What does this mean? You're just a man. We know your parents. You're from Nazareth. What do you mean you're the living bread?"* Bread is the perfect metaphor. In Palestine, it was frequently the only solid food that they ate, the life-giving substance.

Jesus is saying, *"I am your life-giving substance. If you tune in to what I'm saying to you in your life, everything will change."* In your troubles at home, in your troubles at the workplace, in your health issues, the living bread is the presence of the Spirit that will get you through. But the people are not ready to hear that. It is too much. They even ask him, *"What works does God want us to do since you're criticizing us?"* And Jesus responds: *"One work, to believe in the One God sent."* What does that mean? To be receptive to God, to bring into every situation that remembrance of what is revealed to us, what we are told by the Holy One so that everything is transfigured, so that we are able to forgive,

154

we are able to be compassionate, we are able to get past ourselves and our darkness into a new day.

Jesus has to ask them, **"Does this offend you?"** And so I ask you the question of Jesus, does this offend you that he claims to be the ultimate revelation of the nature of God beyond all the wonderful intuitions of cultures and religions? He says: *"You have to feed on my teaching to find your way back to God."* Does this offend you?

And if it does, that is all right. Go your own way, but think of the choice you have just made. Have you walked away from that which is the most life-giving thing you could grab onto? Jesus then makes things worse. He says words like *eat my flesh, drink my blood.* This is all spiritual, signs that point to something else, yet we are constantly taking the signs for the real thing.

To "eat his flesh" is to eat that which he teaches us, that God blesses over-abundantly, that giving thanks is a state of receptivity to Spirit, that out of our simplicity we can help like the little boy. Then, in the midst of our problems, if we place God in the center, we will find resolution.

We are challenged to make this teaching real in your life right now. In our issues, in our events of this day, we are called to make Christ that living bread. He says, **"Those who come to me will never be hungry. Those who believe in me will never be thirsty."** He adds that no one can take us away when we come to him. But notice that you have to be hungry to go to him. If you are satisfied, if you know all you want to know, you do not have the desire to come to him and he cannot fill you. So be hungry, stay hungry for God, stay hungry for that which is good and sacred and you will be fed.

Printed in Great Britain
by Amazon